Insomnia can be cured instantly

Buddhist method to cure insomnia

MYUNGZU KIM

Text Copyright © 2020
Myungzu Kim

All Rights Reserved

Introduction 4

Chapter1. Life principle 18

Chapter 2-Study of the mind to escape insomnia 68

Chapter3, Case Studies of Healing by Life Principle 250

Introduction

Insomnia can definitely be cured. In fact, it can even be cured instantly. There are many such examples at my healing center. How is this possible? The reason is simple. Insomnia is not a disease. Insomnia is just an illusion of sleep, a kind of ignorance that is created by the wrong idea about sleep. If insomnia was a disease, it would take some substantial time to get out, but it does not take that much time to get out of ignorance. As soon as you realize the error of thought, ignorance disappears along with its cause. It is for this reason chronic insomnia can disappear immediately.

But none of those places—hospitals—that claim to cure insomnia tell you this. The reason is simple. They just don't know. There are also many books in the world that insist they can help heal insomnia. However, none of them state that insomnia can disappear the moment you obtain the right thought about sleep. The reason for this is the same. They don't know, either. Why don't they know? Either the writers of these books have never experienced the grueling world of insomnia themselves, or have not dug deep enough into the profound and elaborate principle of the mind that causes insomnia even if they had experienced it.

It is absurd for those who have never suffered from insomnia to say that they know it. It is unquestionable that it's impossible for those who have never suffered from the suffocating pain and despair of insomnia to know how to escape form it completely. It is mostly possible that they got the information from light books on insomnia. It is as if they are saying they can fly a plane and get you safely to a destination after having read a book on aviation just as Lobsang Rampa has said.

I have been through a daunting process until I found out that insomnia can disappear with a single thought. I have also suffered from insomnia myself and almost died from it. I have tried everything other insomniacs have tried, but nothing worked. The realization that there was not a single way out of it in the world was even more frustrating than death itself. However, I became truly determined because I just couldn't choose death. I decided to find the cure to my insomnia myself. It was then that I started searching every nook and cranny for even the slightest clues. Since it was my only way to live, the attempt was fervent and intense. Then, unbelievably, a path to healing appeared and freed me from insomnia. It was the life principle.

The life principle is the principle of the mind. It resembles the process in which all discipliners gain enlightenment. Therefore, if you have freed yourself of insomnia by realizing the life principle, you could say that you have obtained a piece of enlightenment. I have also escaped from insomnia through the life principle and in the process gained a piece of truth. Those who have suffered from insomnia for several years or decades have also experienced the disappearance of insomnia either instantly or gradually depending on their degree of awareness, and at the same time gained Right Views of themselves and of the world. Anyone who believes and follows the life principle of this book will be able to experience the same truth. If you can make the life principle your own, then the percentage of escaping insomnia is 100%.

This book is composed of three parts: (1) the life principle, (2) the study of the mind to escape insomnia, (3) case studies. If you want to get to the core of the healing of insomnia, I suggest you do an intensive reading on the life principle in chapter 1 first. If you are in urgent need to resolve problems such as worries, anxieties and fear, I suggest you read the study of the mind to escape insomnia in chapter 2 first and then come back to read chapter 1 afterwards. Chapter 3 consists of case studies with reasons for their insomnia, their healing process, and their results. Most of them hold stories of instant healing and improvement of insomnia. If you have suffered from insomnia for a long time, this book will make you overwhelmed with joy. You, too, can be healed.

Just like descriptions of a flower cannot replace the flower itself, it is hard to say that my book contains everything about the life principle. However, the content of this book alone may be enough to help you escape from insomnia. In fact, many were healed just by learning partial truths in it. With this book, I look forward to the day when insomnia disappears in the world for good. Since the life principle is a complete solution to insomnia, it is a distinct possibility.

June, 2017

Chapter1. Life principle

1. Insomnia can be cured instantly.

2. Life principle that will cure insomnia

3. Understanding and application of the life principle

4. Clash of the life principle and free will

5. Changes through the awareness of the life principle

6. Practical methods and tips to get rid of insomnia immediately

Chapter 2-Study of the mind to escape insomnia

1. Insomnia cannot be cured immediately?

2. Insomnia and mathematics

3. Dried up well.

4. Effects of gratitude

5. Insomnia is not a fight against sleep.

6. Things you should always remember

7. There is no greater healing power than imagination

8. Medicine for your wounds of insomnia

9. The only thing we should fear is fear itself.

10. Insomnia is a blessing

11. Sleep functions according to the cosmic law

12. The final resting place of insomnia.

13. The waves cannot make winds.

14. Low level healing and the best healing

15. Understanding instead of avoiding

16. Calming the storm of the mind

17. Most effective action for healing insomnia.

18. Insomnia is Murphy's Law?

19. Change your subconscious

20. Mind for healing and Mind for learning

21. Insight or repetition

22. Right Understanding and Attitude toward Stress

23. You should not make contradictory demands.

24. There is a path in the cause

25. Insomnia is but a figment of your imagination

26. When spring blooms in the heart

27. Awareness is a pathway to a new world

28. The Importance of Confidence

29. You heal as much as you desire.

30. Hatred and aversion also cause insomnia.

31. You cannot enter a good university without studying hard

32. Empathize with the Truth

33. Love that can overcome insomnia

34. Will is poison in overcoming Insomnia

35. Night goes, and dawn comes

36. The problem itself is not a problem

37. Peace and calm is your original form.

38. The way to live and the way to die

39. Wisdom not to do what you shouldn't do

40. Always benefit yourself

41. Do not be afraid

42. Enduring mind and understanding mind

43. How to cross the mud patch called sleeping pills

44. I want to sleep a little longer

45. We cannot build a house without a foundation

46. Escape from insomnia has no relationship to time

47. Constant doubt and anxiety

48. Too many cooks spoil the broth.

49. The power to uproot insomnia

50. You think you're wanting and inadequate

51. Street lamp in the dark

52. No self-fulfilling prophecy

53. How to cross the ditch that is insomnia

54. Mistakes may pave the way to healing

55. Problems of waiting for sleep

56. Your self-ego is a wall

57. The key to getting rid of insomnia - who am I?

59. The attitude of a person who thirsts for sleep

60. The mind that calls for sleep

Chapter3, Case Studies of Healing by Life Principle

1. The case of an elementary student (male) whose insomnia disappeared as soon as he heard my words on the life principle spoken by another person

2. A young mother whose insomnia disappeared after only a phone call (woman in her 30's)

3. Meeting of Breathing Law and Life Principle

- Overseas office worker (man in his 50's)

4. Older woman (in her 70's) who recovered from insomnia by thinking of Buddha as the source

5. Is it possible there's something wrong with my brain cells? – university student in his 20's

6. I want to kill myself – office worker in his 40's (male)

7. It is my wish to sleep well just once before I die

(man in his 50's)

8. Sixteen years of insomnia evaporated in one instant – woman in her 30's

9. I know now that it's all about making up your mind - female college student in her 20's

10. It is an unbelievable phenomenon - a civil servant in his 40's (male)

11. It's like magic – insomnia has disappeared.- female office worker in her 30's

12. The body can be changed in one day – office worker for 20 years (female)

Chapter1. Life principle

1. Insomnia can be cured instantly.

Insomnia can be cured or improved instantly. It may seem unbelievable but it is true. However, it is not possible by means of taking medicines, physical exercises, or by drinking teas or consuming foods that help you sleep. This is because Insomnia is a matter of the mind. But many people try to solve the problems of mind through methods unrelated to the mind. All the methods listed above are methods unrelated to the mind. It makes no sense trying to cure problems of the mind through methods unrelated to it. It is useless looking for the key that you lost in your house outside of the house. The solution to curing insomnia rests totally in the mind.

Since insomnia is a matter of the mind and its

solutions rest in the mind, it is neither accident nor miracle that insomnia can be cured instantly and for normal sleep to return. It happens naturally as soon as you change your mind. However, the mind does not change easily. Everyone tells insomniacs to relax their minds and even though they try very hard to do so, their minds are not easily relaxed. The more they try to relax the mind the deeper they fall into despair and suffer from pain.

The way to change your mind lies elsewhere. It is to become aware of the principles of sleep. It is to become aware of the life principle that is the basis of the principles of sleep. When you become aware of life principle, you become aware of the sleep principle, become sympathetic to the truth of the principles of sleep, and the mind that was so difficult to change changes by itself. This is the right way to change the mind.

If you do not know this truth, it is difficult to change your wrongful mind and thoughts, and any chance of instant cure of insomnia will be gone. This is why people say insomnia is difficult to cure and long term insomnia is harder to cure still. Therefore curing or improving the conditions of insomnia requires a precondition.

That precondition is to become aware of the life principle and to follow them. If you believe and follow the life principle, and if you have no reservations or doubts about this principle being the truth, then there is little doubt that your conditions of insomnia will disappear instantly no matter how long you have suffered from it, or at least improve drastically. Such statement has been proven by numerous people that came to my healing center who have been either instantly cured or had drastic improvements of insomnia regardless of the time they had insomnia.

At first, these people did not come with such expectations. They came to the Center out of desperation after having exhausted all options including visiting various hospitals to cure insomnia. But these skeptical people that came to the center became aware of the life principle through consultations with me and were totally amazed by the healing effects on insomnia. If such person is one, two, three, four... but over ten, then it proves that healing insomnia by the life principle is not accidental and that it can be applied to all.

Whoever you are, no matter how long you have suffered from insomnia, the moment you become aware of the life principle and the truths of the life principle are firmly entrenched in your heart, then insomnia will automatically disappear and you can return to normal sleep. It is like turning on the light switch in a dark room. No matter how long the room has been dark, it immediately becomes bright as soon as it is lit. Insomnia is the same. No matter how long your mind room of Insomnia has been kept in the dark, the moment that the light of the life principle is lit, the darkness of insomnia disappears in a flash.

The reason why insomnia can be cured instantly is because you have changed in that instant. When we change, the world around us changes. This is the only and the easiest way to change the world we live in. But if we do not change, it is impossible for our world to change. A changed world does not come to us with open arms when we stay still. Therefore, if you want to change your world of insomnia, you must change. That is, your mind must change. This is the only and the easiest way to escape the world of insomnia

The point of conversion is consciousness. If your consciousness of sleep changes dramatically, your insomnia will change dramatically. If your consciousness of sleep is not easily changed or takes its time in changing, then your insomnia does not improve or will take time in healing. Your awareness of the life principle is the key. As soon as you become aware of the life principle of sleep and that awareness goes to your heart, all the fears and anxieties stemming from insomnia will vanish like a mirage. The fact that insomnia vanishes instantly is an extra bonus.

2. Life principle that will cure insomnia

The universe is a life form. The movement of the universe is due to its life functions. The movement of the stars, the rotation of the earth, the maintenance of life of plants and animals to humans is all possible through life functions. And at the base of these life functions exist the life principle.

Whether visible or not, whether we know it or not, if something functions it means there is a principle to that function. A cellular phone functions based on principles and it is impossible for that cellular phone to work against its functioning principles. If there are basic principles that guide the functions even for manmade electronics, there can be no doubt that there are guiding principles in the movement of the universe.

In other words, the existence of a life function means that life principle exists. Whether it is a star, a person, an animal or a plant, all lives are driven by the life principle and no lives exist contrary to it.

Since the universe that is equal to life functions according to the life principle and the sleep that is equal to life function also functions according to the life principle, then the life principle itself is the principle of the universe and the principle of sleep. For instance, the principle of falling asleep and waking up is the same as the functioning of our bodies, and of the sun rising and falling as well as the movement of the stars. If you think about it, our body is just a smaller scale of the universe and ultimately there is no real difference between the universe and our body.

This life principle governs the life functions of the

universe within each of us and controls the areas of life that our consciousness cannot intervene. For example, we can chew rice, but we cannot intervene in the digestion of food. No matter how hard you try, your thoughts and will have no control over the food once it goes through the throat and falls into an area that we have no control over. People gave this area of no control the name of "autonomic nerve". Although we, as in our brain, have no control over the digestive process of excreting digestive acid and the movement of our stomach, but nonetheless are completed automatically, hence the term "autonomic nerve" has been coined.

But the term "autonomy" has a connotation of our ignorance. Since we have no idea why food is digested by itself, we call it "autonomy". As our lungs breathe and our hearts beat by themselves, and thus these functions also share the word "autonomy". I guess that the word "autonomy" can explain the automatic nature of these functions but it also reflects our ignorance of not knowing the true nature of these functions.

As mentioned before, even man-made crude electronic products function under the operating principles created by their creators, and to think that a complex life form such as a human being functioning autonomously without any guiding principles is absurd.

There is no 'autonomy' in the universe. The universe moves according to its guiding principles. The fact that there are guiding principles means that there is a subject that devised it. The guiding principles are not made by itself without its maker. We have coined the names such as the Creator, the Heroine, the God, the Root, the Source, and so on.

But the name itself is not so important. It is literally just a name and not the substance. But we know this: there is some force in the universe that we don't know of and that through this force the universe operates and life thrives.

I will try to explain the life principle in an easier way. In the beginning there was a seed. In certain instant when the temperature and humidity was just right, the seed started to spread its roots and grew to be a tall tree with numerous branches and countless leaves. The tree took the form of roots, branches and leaves, and the countless leaves receive nutrients through the branches that are sent by the roots.

This is similar to how the universe operates. The universe is made up of countless lives created from the source, all of which are interconnected to the source by invisible energy field. Even a single dust, even all the animals and plants, even the human beings, even the stars in the sky, all living beings live and operate through the energy of the universal source.

The fact that all life forms live by the power of the source is like saying I too do not live by my will but through the power of the source. The heart beats not by my will but by the power of the source. Sleep is the same. Sleep and heartbeat are the same life functions and these functions are what the source controls. All our life functions are the same. The life principle is the interrelationship between the source and the life.

3. Understanding and application of life principle

Although the universe moves by the life principle, the force that causes the movement is invisible. The motions of the moving star can be seen, but the force that moves the star is invisible. The sun rises and sets, but the force that rotates the earth cannot be seen. The movement of the body can be seen, but the force that moves the body cannot. We can see people sleeping and waking up but the force that allows us to sleep and wake up cannot be seen.

However, although we cannot see the force, we know its existence. It is much like knowing that there is wind through the flapping of flags although we can't see the wind itself, and although we can't actually see electricity we know there is electricity by the light bulb lighting up when we turn on the switch. The fact that there is some reaction means that there is some force activating the reaction. Life functions are operated by a force. That force is life force and the subject of the force is the source of the universe.

The source of the universe cares for all lives. That care is as perfect as God is perfect, as harmonious as God is harmonious, and as balanced as God is balanced. Even though we ourselves may not care, the source takes care of the universe, the nature and us through its perfection. It is also the work of the source that makes you sleep and wake up. Therefore, it is ridiculous for you to say that you have insomnia and that you suffer from it.

It is a comedy to say that you are suffering because you cannot fall asleep, because it is the work of the source that you sleep, not yours. Are you suffering from insomnia now? Then you are now performing a perfect comedy.

Sleeping and waking up are no different from rising and setting of the sun. It is unreasonable to control your sleep with your thoughts and will as much as it is unreasonable to use your thoughts and will to move the sun and the moon. Just as it is impossible to pick the stars off the sky, the only price of your personal greed for sleep will be despair and frustration.

Are you now in a state of desperation due to insomnia? You need not be. It is not that difficult to rid yourself of insomnia. It is simpler than you think. You need only to admit your limitations. You just have to admit that you do not have control over your sleep. Are you asking if that admission is difficult? No it isn't. Such admissions are simple. Your admission will be automatic as soon as you realize that your sleep cannot be controlled by your thoughts and will and your attempts to control your sleep through your thoughts and mind is futile.

Any cure of insomnia starts with your complete awareness that you cannot control sleep. Sleep is controlled by the life principle. Just as the roots take care of the tree, the source takes care of all life and life functions that are connected to the source. As soon as you become aware of these principles about the source, you begin to realize that what you have known about sleep is fundamentally wrong and your worries, anxieties and fear begin to fade away. And at the same time, insomnia will disappear. Your awareness of these principles is indispensable prerequisite for resolving insomnia.

Let me reiterate. You sleep and wake up according to the life forces of the source. It is the source that takes care of sleep, so you do not have to worry nor do you have to do anything. Knowing this fact is to attain complete awareness of the life principle and a right attitude towards sleep.

If you know the source and know what it does, does this knowledge alone cure insomnia? Not necessarily. This is because you may think you know the source but you may not know it correctly. Much like you think you know true love but it may not be true love. Love is completed by the addition of faith. You may think you love someone but if you lack the faith, then that is not true love. Likewise, knowledge without faith in the source is not true knowledge. Knowledge without the faith is the knowledge in your brain and such knowledge does not help in the cure of insomnia.

Our realization that it is not ourselves that control sleep, and our belief in our mind that it is the source that looks after our sleep; these are what will complete the awareness and knowledge. Such awareness is what will relieve us from the worries and anxieties and cure insomnia.

Everybody has different reactions. According to my experience, people with faster understanding tended to develop the awareness faster and cure faster. For people with developed emotions, faith was a more important factor. But when understanding and faith were combined, the healing effects became most effective.

Insomnia is an illusion created by wrong ideas, but when that illusion is accepted as the truth, the illusion becomes a powerful force. It may even imprison you for the rest of your life. However, when it is faced with correct awareness and faith, such illusion will crumble like a house of cards. This is how decades long insomnia can disappear in an instant. When you have such awareness and faith, it is impossible for you to have insomnia.

4. Clash of life principle and free will

You now know that the life function of sleep is beyond the realm of human thought and will. You also know that sleep is controlled by life functions much the same way as the movement of stars, the movement of the earth and the blossoming of flowers. Nevertheless, you may still try to exert your faint thoughts and will for sleeping.

Although you don't think that you can control the same life functions such as the movement of stars, the rotation of earth and the blossoming of flowers and would never try to use your will to change them, when it comes to sleep, the moment sleep becomes irregular, worries and anxieties creep in and you may try to manipulate it through other efforts. You might try taking some pills or resort to consuming alcohol and/or other attempts to help you in getting a good night's sleep.

This irony contains a truth that needs your attention. Although our thoughts and will have no influence in altering the movement of stars, the rotation of sun and the moon, the changing of seasons, or the blooming of flowers, when it comes to life areas of self-ego, our thoughts and will can influence it. In other words, when it comes to life functions of the human body, our thoughts and will can exert some influence, particularly in the negative sense.

For example, although sleep is a perfect universal life function and we cannot control it, if we have negative thoughts such as worry, anxiety, and fear for sleep, the life functions working harmoniously in our body gets twisted and distorted because of such worries, anxieties and fears.

This can be proven by the experiences of insomniacs. The fact that one day of sleepless night and the ensuing worries and anxieties about sleeping develops into insomnia and other sleep disorders clearly shows us that it is our negative thoughts and will that affect our life functions. This is how a perfectly operating nature can lose its order and equilibrium as soon as humans try to interfere with the system. That is why these insomniacs are paying the price of suffering by interfering with life functions with negative thoughts, and this is entirely their fault.

When you reach this point, one question surfaces: how is it that the life functions of other natural objects, such as stars, moon, tree, grass and others are never affected by our thoughts and wills, but can have negative impacts on the life functions of our bodies?

If all lives in the universe work on the same life principle, then shouldn't our sleep which is a part of life functions of our body operate harmoniously regardless of our thoughts and will? This difference is due to the function of free will which is unique to human beings, and affects us only in negative ways.

Free will is the gift God gave to man and it is through this free will that we acquire value and meaning as human beings. Human being without any will has no value and meaning of being a human. A person with no will to do anything has no meaning to be born and such a person cannot be born. It is as if a person who has no intention of learning will not go to school. Therefore, our free will is not only the proof that we came to earth with a purpose, but also the necessary and sufficient condition for being humans.

But the free will which is a necessary and sufficient condition for being humans is a double-edged sword. It is emancipation as well as a shackle. Free will allows us to accomplish many things but also can become an obstacle. For example, when we cannot accomplish what we want even though we try our best, then free will does not function as a tool for liberation but a cauldron of pain.

There is no bigger suffering than exerting your will to which are impossible to obtain. Everybody will experience such limits to free will at least once in his or her lifetime. And even though nobody asked them to, they will abandon the effort.

It is a human task to try hard, but the results are always determined by the heaven. Although farmers work hard on tilling the land, the fruits of the labor are determined by God. The runner may run hard, but his record is not determined by his will. Those who have lived a long life with many experiences come to realize that trying one's best and waiting for the result without greed is the best wisdom in life. Once you accept this as the motto of your life, you begin to realize that your will is actually a stumbling block in life and that your only choice is to abandon it.

Only when I lay down my thoughts and my will and accept the principles of God, my soul will grow naturally. The moment I lay down my will, the moment I accept God's hand in everything I do, I rid myself of the limits of human beings and soar above. If you experienced everything that can be achieved through free will, letting go of your free will will let you enter into the realm of God. This is the hidden truth behind the free will that God has bestowed upon us.

The fact that a problem was created in the life area of sleep reflects that you reached a stage in your life where you must let go of your free will and need to develop your soul. Therefore, your sleep disorder is not a product of collision between life function and free will. It is a sign that old world is over and you move onto a new world. This is a path from a physical world to the new world of soul. It is a manifestation of a blessing.

In order to return to the original order of sleep, insomniacs should learn "without self" to put down the free will. Learning "without self" is to do nothing. Life function is a realm of doing nothing. It is the realm of God. If you succeed in sleeping normally by laying down your will for sleep, then it means you have just escaped the world of self and entered a new world of "without self". It means you have left the realm of humans and entered a new realm of Gods. That is why your experience of insomnia is truly a blessing.

5. Changes through the awareness of life principle

During the pure days of childhood, you did not have any thoughts or will for life function of sleep. When it was time to go to bed, you used to go to bed and sleep. You did not have any greed for sleep or any obsessions about it. Just as you would not have any greed for sun, moon and stars, you have maintained similar attitude regarding sleep. That is exactly why you never had problems with sleep.

But one day, for some reason you stayed up all night and your worries and anxieties about sleep began to wield its ugly head. Since then you became conscious of sleeping, began worrying about it and fearful about not being able to fall asleep and insomnia became a painful shadow that you cannot shake off. The more you worried about sleep, the harder the pain became. What others never experience, such natural life function of sleep became pain and suffering for you. As soon as you became conscious about sleep, such changes occurred.

This change is comparable to going back to the womb to be born again. It is comparable to a grain of wheat rotting to sprout again. It is comparable to experiencing death. However, it will not be easy for you to die. Every time you face death, being a creature of habit, you will violently resist death. Since you have never had such thoughts, since you always thought that you can control sleep, the thought of letting go of your will to control the life function of sleep will seem like suicide. However, ultimately you will let go of your will and accept the natural laws of sleep similar to accepting the natural laws of nature. Since this is the only road to normal sleep, it is the only choice left to you.

In the process, it is inevitable that you will undergo some changes. The process is painful. Changes are always accompanied by pain. There is pain in the change from cocoon to butterfly. There is pain in the process of becoming a new self. If the change is small, the pain is small. If the change is big, the pain is big. If a person undergoes a complete transformation overnight, then it is very likely that he experienced tremendous and unimaginable pain. Insomnia is such a pain.

The pain of insomnia is like tasting death while living. Anybody will be shaken by such experience. That is how cruel and unforgiving the pain is. Nobody would welcome such pain. However, such pain is the will of God that you be reborn. If that was not the case, the pain would not have come to you.

There is no such a thing as coincidence in the universe and if an indescribable pain found its way to you, then it is only logical to view this opportunity as a gift from God that you be reborn – to transform yourself into a new being, instead of an unlucky coincidence. Actually, the insomniacs who escaped the condition through the acceptance of the life principle have transformed into new beings. The transformation was an existential leap.

We all have seeds of Buddha but it is difficult to germinate this seed. It is not easy to succeed in putting down myself due to the solid wall of self-ego. If you think about it, our lives are but a life of grain of wheat. However, if the conditions are right, that grain of wheat will sprout and will reap golden harvest.

Likewise, insomniacs can escape from the prison

of self-ego, once they realize that they do not control sleep. That realization is comparable to finding the seed of Buddha from within and watering it and germinating it. Therefore if a person was able to beat insomnia through the realization of the life principle, then it is comparable to experiencing the universal nature of Buddha without even knowing it.

There was a man who told me that he cannot sleep when away from home. He was suffering from intense insomnia. The fear and anxiety from insomnia was so severe that his mental health was seriously damaged. To him, the thought of leaving his home and sleeping was an impossibility. Leaving home meant that he must spend long nights totally awake. However, he became aware of the life principle through consultations and the fear and anxiety of sleep disappeared from his mind and the next day found himself sleeping soundly in someone else's home. The difference between realizing the life principle and not realizing it is that much great.

Do you have insomnia now? Do you find that sleeping somewhere other than your home is much more difficult? Life principle can solve that problem. If you are aware of the life principle and embrace it, you will be comfortable wherever you are. Even if the earth is to split into two tomorrow, you can sleep comfortably today. Sleep in a state of awareness of the life principle is like promissory notes guaranteed to be paid.

6. Practical methods and tips to get rid of insomnia immediately

I have already outlined that insomnia can be cured or improved instantly through awareness and belief in the life principle. I have also outlined that such statements are not just mere claims or slogans but real life examples. If you are an insomniac, if the conditions are rooted in the mind, then you can also experience the same results. However, even though you may have attained the awareness and faith of the life principle, you must verify if such awareness is correct. In other words, your awareness of the life principle may just be an understanding occurring in your head.

The awareness that is not in the heart but in the head has no healing power. It is comparable to a flower in a painting having no characteristics of a real flower. Therefore, you must verify if your awareness is of the heart and not of the head. The head understands but the heart feels. If your awareness of the life principle is felt, then the awareness stems from the heart. Such awareness automatically leads to faith. Therefore it is only natural that your insomnia will dramatically be cured.

The following is a practical task and practices that you should try at least for immediate relief of insomnia if not a downright cure of insomnia. If you have been turning the pages too fast in your haste and missed some important points in this book, then this is an opportunity to catch up. You must reflect on each of practices below. If your study is going well, it means that your condition has a good chance to be healed or improved.

Practice 1-Rid yourself of the expectations to be healed.

"What are you talking about? You told us that insomnia can be cured in an instant and now you tell us not to expect insomnia to be healed at all?" This is an obvious response. You may say to yourself that is contradiction in terms. But this statement is neither wrong nor contradictory. If your wish is to rid yourself of insomnia, and to rid yourself right away, then you really cannot expect such cure to be possible.

No matter how the changes derived from the awareness is true, if your expectations to rid yourself of insomnia and that "this should be enough to cure my insomnia" is present in your mind, then the chances of your curing insomnia diminishes drastically. When your expectations include "immediate cure" then the probability of curing insomnia is close to zero. What am I talking about? If your expectations about sleep include these thoughts then the chances of cure has the opposite effect. What do I mean by that?

Expectation is an approximation of the future. The results of expectations are that it may or it may not come true. For example, we may plan for a picnic tomorrow and may hope that it will not rain. However, we can never be sure that it will not rain tomorrow. Similarly, even if we were to accept the life principle and hope for your dear life that such expectations will truly free you from insomnia, it means that you currently possess anxieties that such hope may actually not come true.

If you have suffered from insomnia for a long time and your anxieties have been great then such possibilities are even greater. If your expectation and your anxieties about sleep are present at the same time, then the possibilities of your insomnia being cured is zero.

The life principle is the complete answer required to cure insomnia. There cannot be any doubts. However, conversely, you should never expect such results. No matter how true your awareness of the life principle is the fundamental truth required to curing insomnia, you should not expect the results. What would happen if the result does not meet my expectations? You will be devastated. It would be like rejoicing the freedom from prison only to be imprisoned again.

Practice 2-Holding onto the Truth of the Life Principle

Now that you learnt that your crude expectation to be cured of insomnia is wrong and a no-no, it should be apparent to you that the only way out is for you to accept the life principle. What is the way to hold on to the truths? That is to feel the truth through your heart instead of understanding it through your brain. "That's right! This is the truth" "This is the way!" Such thoughts may seem like knowing the life principle, but if your feelings for such knowledge are weak, then it may be a sign that your awareness of the truth of the life principle is insufficient.

If such is the case, then you must make concerted efforts to learn the life principle by heart. You must try to feel the lungs breathing and heart beating without the intervention of your thoughts and will. You must feel it wholeheartedly. "My heart beating is outside my control." "My lungs breathing air in and out of my body is being controlled by the source and so is sleeping" You need to repeat these thoughts. If these thoughts get etched in your heart, if these truths echo through your heart, then normal sleep will be realized.

Practice 3-Do not be disappointed or suspicious

After believing that you have gained this knowledge and faith about life principle and yet the symptoms of insomnia persist, you must not be disappointed and complain that the theory of the life principle is bogus or fake. You should never complain or doubt of its truthfulness.

There are no problems in the life principle. All your life functions are still driven by them. The beating of your heart and the breathing of your lungs are still beyond your control, and they do so regardless of your intent.

They do the work because of the nature of their design. Just as the universe filled with lives works in harmony, the life functions of your body universe is always harmonious, and operate without any interventions from you. You must continue to believe that these principles work unconditionally without your interference. If your belief and awareness become unconditional and complete, then your life functions will surely kick in and the cure for insomnia will certainly be obtained.

Therefore, if your insomnia does not disappear or is not improved, it is not because there is a problem with the life principle, it is because there is a problem with your awareness and belief in the life principle. In any case, what you need to do is not to be disappointed or suspicious about the life principle, but to fully awaken your awareness and belief in it.

When the awareness and belief of the life principle reach perfection, the vital functions of the body universe become perfect. Just as the heart beats perfectly and digestion is performed without problems, you will sleep and wake up perfectly. Under no circumstances should you be disappointed or suspicious of the life principle. The life principle is the personification of God. It is harmonious without question. The people with such faith have all healed without the use of medicine. There is no reason to believe that you are the exception to the rule.

Practice 4-Checking yourself with worry and anxiety

If the awareness and belief of life functions and

their subject are firmly established, if there is no disappointment and doubt about it, it can be said that the awareness and belief of the vital functions and their principle are complete. In other words, if you feel that it is "right" in your heart rather than think "I understand" in your head, your awareness and belief in the vital functions and life principle are complete.

But you may not be totally sure that it is really perfect and complete. Even if we are fully aware and believe that life functions are the work of the source and that the source is fully responsible for taking care of our life functions, measuring the depth of our belief is no easy feat. Similar to how Peter who was sure that he would never deny Jesus Christ denied Jesus three times without knowing himself, we may not fully know our true selves.

However, the verification of your awareness and belief in sleep that is the universal life function is surprisingly easy. They are easily verified by a litmus test of worry and anxiety. What does this mean? Is it possible to verify my awareness and belief in the life functions by my worry and anxiety? But this is not as farfetched as it sounds. If your awareness and belief are correct and complete, no worries and anxiety of sleep will occur under any circumstances.

On the contrary, if there are holes in your awareness and belief in the life principle, the worries and anxieties about sleep will reappear. If you are still worried and anxious about sleep even though you are aware of the life principle, then it is proof that your knowledge and faith in the life principle are incomplete.

This is how your worries and anxieties on sleep

reveal how deeply rooted your knowledge and faith in the life principle are within you. This is also how you can use this test to confirm the status of your awareness. If you do not have an inkling of worries and anxieties about sleep, your awareness and faith are complete.

However, if there is even a tiniest bit of worries and anxieties still present, then you still possess the roots of insomnia within you. Then you must return to your studies. You must feel the heart beating and how such same life function is responsible for your sleep to rid yourself of worries and anxieties about sleep. You must repeat this exercise until your worries and anxieties disappear.

Practice 5-Be aware that I cannot heal my own

insomnia.

The life of a leaf is dependent on the root, not on the leaf itself. No matter how healthy the leaf, if it is cut off its roots, the leaf cannot survive. My life is also dependent on the source and not on myself. The life functions of my body are also the work of the source. Just as the leaf was not able to cure its fate itself, insomnia cannot be cured by my efforts.

Just as the leaf had no power to heal itself, I have no power to heal my insomnia. Efforts of the leaf cannot overcome its fate by itself. My personal efforts cannot heal my insomnia. This awareness is what you must have in order to cure insomnia.

Practice 6-Recognizing the subject of life functions

Even though I do nothing, the life functions of my

body, such as sleeping, breathing and heartbeat......operate in harmony. We may call this autonomic nervous system, but this is only an expression of human ignorance that we do not know how the system operates. The fact that there is function means that there is a guiding principle and that there is a subject that controls it.

There is a subject in the movement of the universe, in the movement of nature, in my life functions. It is the source of the universe. Much like the leaf was connected to the root and lived by the energy of the root, I too am connected to the source and live by the power of the source. All humans and their vital functions, such as sleeping, breathing, and the beating of the hearts, have the power of the source as the subject. Once you grasp the idea and embrace it to be the truth, then you can rest assured. Knowing that the source takes care of all life functions will ease your worries and anxieties.

Practice 7-Accepting vitality

We are not 100% open to the vitality of the source. If we were to be 100% open to the vitality of the source, even eternal life would be possible. We are open to the vitality only to the extent that we can be alive and slowly grow old. As time goes by, our breathing and heart beat will decline and eventually stop. But until we face death, the vitality we accept is enough to sustain us during our lifetime.

We also never worry about such life functions. However, if sleeping is irregular, it means that there is a problem with the functioning of the area of sleep and that the function of the life force is not perfect in the area. What I need to do in order to rectify the situation is to let the source take control of my mind. That is to completely entrust in the source that it will allow me to return to my normal sleep. Such acceptance in the source is the force that is required to propel the life force within.

Sleeping Tips

① Upon going to bed and laying yourself down to sleep, what you need to do now is to remind yourself that it is the source that will allow sleep to come. Your repeated awareness of the life principle is the tool required in obtaining good night's sleep.

② The repeated mistakes accumulated by bad habits may bring about worries and anxieties on sleep unconsciously. At such times, you must realize it immediately and assure yourself that the source is the underlying force that can bring sleep to you. In other words, you must repeat to yourself that "this is wrong." "It is not me that controls sleep, but the work of the source." "Just as the roots take care of the tree, the source will take care of me."

③ If your awareness and faith in the principle of life remain unchanged, you begin to be conscious of your breathing. This does not mean you become conscious of your breathing per se, but that you become aware of it. It doesn't matter if it takes one hour two hours or even if you spend the whole night. You just allow the source to take control of sleep and spend the time noticing your each breath.

This completes what you need to do at bedtime. The rest is taken care of by the source. Whether it makes you sleep or not, it is the role of the source that controls the universe. All you need to do is to put yourself in the hands of the source much like a baby would allow itself in the hands of its mother. Complete trust begets complete care.

Chapter 2-Study of the mind to escape insomnia

I was able to rid myself of insomnia after the realization of the life principle. People who have been suffering insomnia for many years or even many decades all were relieved of insomnia through the realization of the life principle. No medications, no expensive prescriptions or tests, no cumbersome food or exercises were required.

For some people the cure was immediate and for others it took them longer, but they all shared the same underlying principle that they all escaped insomnia through the awareness of the life principle. Even those that were taking sleeping pills, the only difference was that it took them longer to wean out of their dependence on the drugs, but shared the same experience of ridding

insomnia.

If you were to become aware of the life principle and follow the principles faithfully, you too can experience such truths. However, for you to hold onto one truth alone in the course of your life, the world of mind is way more complex and difficult. Every time you face storms of the mind it is not sufficient that your boat is strong and safe. You also require a wise and safe helm to steer your way out of the storm that strikes your heart from time to time. Your "study of the mind to escape insomnia" is a helm in the mind to steer out from those moments that storms in the mind strike wisely and safely.

This is a wise method of overcoming the storms of the mind such as worries, anxieties, fears, wonderments, conflicts, irritations, and frustrations you may experience unconsciously while suffering insomnia. When you experience such storms of the mind, look up this book for related titles and read the passages. If you read them with truly open mind, you will notice that the storm of your mind will subside and find a solution from within.

These passages will calm the storm of your mind and act as the veteran captain that can guide you out of the storm.   With its guidance, you will be able to find clues to resolving the wild storms of insomnia and be able to light the lighthouse that will guide you in the darkness of your mind.

For that reason, you should never skim through these pages lightly. Similar to how you would start drawing a picture on a canvas, you should carefully etch the truths into your mind. The point is in the depth of reading not in the speed. If you are able to adopt at least one paragraph you can sympathize with as your own, that single paragraph may be the key in resolving insomnia.

1. Insomnia cannot be cured immediately?

Yesterday is never the same as today as today is never the same as yesterday. Nobody knows what will transpire overnight. Nobody can be certain that the insomnia I had yesterday can never be healed overnight. Of course such occurrence cannot happen by itself. There is no instance where God will reach out to you while you remain idle. In order for insomnia to disappear overnight, you have to change. Alas, changing yourself is no easy feat. Your old thoughts will resist you every step of the way.

But the moment you encounter the truth of the life principle, you are automatically changed. When the truth of the life principle is carved into your heart, your old thoughts are automatically erased. Let yourself float over flowing water like the fallen leaves, let yourself be cleared by the wind along with the clouds in the sky. All you have to do is to entrust yourself to the flow of life. The moment you entrust yourself to the flow of life, anything that goes against this flow such as insomnia will disappear automatically.

Many people escaped insomnia through these methods. Some immediately, some quite fast though not immediately, but all saw improvements. Life principals are the same for everyone and therefore there were no exceptions to the rule. However, in order to achieve these results you must get rid of the old and useless ideas about sleep and any reliance and obsession on these decrepit ideas must be boldly abandoned.

Your only course of action is your awareness and faith on the life principle. This is how your life functions will return to normal.

"Can I truly achieve this?" Such a question is absolutely unnecessary.

Of course, it may be difficult to believe without the experience. Since the world we live in is filled with deceit and hypocrisy, it is only wise to be cautious of blind faiths. However, when there are numerous people who have been cured through the awareness of the life principle and are available to you as proof, it would be more foolish not to believe it.

2. Insomnia and mathematics

There are countless math problems in the world. And there are certain formulas absolutely necessary to solve the problems.

Of course, there are times when the problems are solved by accident. We all had such experiences during our school days where we were able to solve a problem accidentally without understanding how we derived the answer. However, such accidental solution does not guarantee that we will solve similar questions when we encounter them again.

Accidents can happen but very unlikely the same accident will happen twice. The inspiration we had to solve the problem may not present itself again. However, if we had the correct formula to solve the problem in the first place, we would be able to solve similar problems over and over again without much difficulty.

This likewise also applies to insomnia. There are times when the pain and suffering of insomnia disappears by chance only to reappear again. However, this time insomnia persists unlike the last time. You try to replicate how you managed to get rid of it the last time but somehow it persists.

Total cure of insomnia cannot be obtained by accident. It is difficult to solve insomnia by trying one solution today that may have worked yesterday or random methods that may have worked for some other times. Just as a math problem has a unique formula for solving the problem, insomnia also must be tackled using the formula that will fundamentally cure the problem.

Insomnia caused by the sickness of the body must

be cured by curing the sickened body. Insomnia caused by the sickness of the mind must be cured by curing the sickened mind.

3. Dried up well.

People do not dig randomly to find wells. They use dowsing to locate underground water. The work of digging is conducted only after locating the underground water source. When no such evidence is found, digging randomly would be foolish.

When no evidence of water exists, then it means there is no water underground and the only answer is to look elsewhere.

You must approach insomnia the same way. If you were unsuccessful in your attempts at curing insomnia, then you should stop the methods that you have been using to cure it. Repeated attempts using the same method is futile. What is now important is your decision. If your repeated attempts to cure insomnia have been unsuccessful, then you must bravely abandon such attempts determining that your attempts are not the solution to the cure.

It is a hasty judgment to conclude that just because your hole in the ground does not produce water, other wells would be the same. Just because you were not able to cure insomnia, it would be a hasty judgment to conclude insomnia is an incurable disease.

Just as there is plentiful underground water, there is always a cure for insomnia. However, just as digging for any holes in the ground would not yield water, you must stop your unsuccessful attempts to cure insomnia.

4. Effects of gratitude

Even insomniacs sleep from time to time. However, the amount of sleep they get is not enough to satiate their need for sleep and such deprivation of sleep further increases their thirst and dissatisfaction resulting in chronic insomnia.

However, instead of suffering from the lack of sleep, if you were to realize that you were able to catch at least some sleep and embrace the grateful attitude, your body and mind will relax some of the stress, creating conditions that will allow further sleep and accelerate the curing process of insomnia.

It is surprisingly easy to be grateful for sleep. No matter the amount of sleep you were able to have, gratitude for sleep requires no special effort or struggle.

However, the effects of gratitude are enormous. Many people conquered the great mountains of insomnia by ridding themselves of the thirst and greed for sleep, and instead, using the grateful mind for sleep.

The time when you need the gratitude for sleep most is when your greed for sleep is at its highest. You will find strange transformation of your mind when you stop your irritations from lack of sleep and embrace the gratitude for sleep however short it may have been. Such strange transformation represents your mind of stress changing to mind of calmness. The calm mind is the secret recipe required to cure insomnia.

5. Insomnia is not a fight against sleep.

Insomnia is not a fight against sleep. If life is a long journey, insomnia is the most difficult and arduous leg of that journey.

In your journey of insomnia, you will encounter unbearable and maximum pain imaginable. In that experience, there will be nobody that can offer you a hand of assistance no matter how hard you may suffer. People around you will merely continue with their journeys unaware of your sleep deprivation, your hardship and the reasons for your cries. That is how insomnia will make you face absolute solitude.

There is nobody there. You cannot rely on anybody. No one is there to help you. There is only you and you alone.

On this lonesome journey of insomnia, the journey

where no one is there to help and every hardship must be tackled alone, you will encounter God. There and then you will let go of yourself and rely totally on God. There is no other alternative. You never had any control over sleep in the first place so letting go of all your feelings, thoughts, anxieties and fears about sleep, you let God take total control over sleep.

In the process of letting go of all your control over sleep, instead of feeling frustration and desperation, you will experience strange sense of peace of mind. Your mind that had been suffering from the pain of insomnia will suddenly find peace and calm.

In that calm and peace, you come to realize that man is a part of nature and the harmony and balance of nature is exactly the same balance and harmony of the body and mind. Therefore your obsession for sleep disappears. There can be no worries and anxieties of sleep in the minds of people who have the realization that there is nature's harmony and balance within the body and mind.

Knowing the truth you would not have realized if not for insomnia, your soul will undergo a maturing transformation that you could never even dreamt of, if you had not taken the journey of insomnia.

Insomnia is not a fight against sleep. It is the rare self-realization of your deep blue soul and God becoming one through the experience of pain and difficulties of life.

6. Things you should always remember

Life is a sea and you are the captain of a ship that sails over the vast sea. It is up to you to steer the ship through good weather and bad, and through countless variables you encounter during your sail.

When you encounter a dangerous storm, your decisions will decide whether your ship will endure the storm or succumb to it and sink.

It is not an over-exaggeration to say that insomnia is the biggest storm you can face during your life's journey in the sea. The pains of insomnia will suffocate you, driving you to the extreme state of mind without a resting place, ultimately to the point of inescapable mental panic attacks.

Many people who face the storm of insomnia fail to survive the storm harmlessly. Such is the force and danger of the storm. No matter how clever and brilliant, when sleep is deprived and cannot find sleep no matter how much you struggle, in such a state, finding rational and wise decision is not easy. Like being stranded in the middle of a desert without any guidelines of directions and not knowing the whereabouts of a shelter, self-control in such a state is tantamount to impossible.

But no matter how scary the storm and how difficult the pain is to endure, it is never beyond the realm of our endurance to overcome it. It is as no matter how dark a night is a new day will eventually come, and no matter how cold a winter and how hot the summer, the seasons will inevitably follow the laws of nature.

However, when we are ignorant of this universal balance and order within our suffering, we exaggerate the size of the storm and treat it as a formidable power that cannot be overcome and make the mistake of becoming desperate, losing any hope of overcoming the storm of insomnia. Such despair is much more dangerous than insomnia itself. A person without hope has no escape plan. For people with only self-pity and despair without a will, to fight even a pebble, can become an obstacle as big as a cliff.

Therefore, as the captain of the ship sailing through the seas of life, you must always remember: The universe is always in harmony with order. Your body universe is also in order and harmony and any storm of life cannot sink you, as long as you do not fall into despair.

7. There is no greater healing power than imagination

The power of imagination is great in overcoming insomnia. In the cure of insomnia, the power of imagination has much greater power than other attempts or will that people commonly use to cure insomnia.

You probably already experienced how insomnia persists no matter how much you try and exert your will. But the power of imagination is different.

If you stop your efforts and use your limitless power of imagination, you will be amazed at how easy it is to overcome insomnia.

You probably are asking yourself: "Imagination?" "How could imagination be so effective?" "Isn't imagination just a thought?"

Although imagination may fall under the category of thought, it is different than normal thought. While the subjects of thought rest in present consciousness, the subjects of imagination are concerned with possibilities of present consciousness. For example, while your consciousness of beauty at looking at a bridge is thought, your fear that the bridge may collapse by a tsunami or that a person may jump off the bridge is imagination.

The power of imagination is great. It is the power to achieve desired future. If you have undeniable optimistic imagination about the future of your sleep, it is only natural that the forces of insomnia will fade away and you will achieve normal sleep.

Therefore, while your will is something you must avoid in curing insomnia, your imagination is indispensable in combatting it.

Imagination doesn't just happen. Imagination grows with your faith and trust of the subjects of your imagination. When you have faith and trust in your imagination, then your future will bloom with fresh healthy flowers. However, if you have doubts and suspicions about your imagination, then instead of your future blooming with bright flowers, your future will wither like flowers without water.

Now it should be much clearer to you as to what you need to do to cure insomnia.

From this moment on, you with insomnia should constantly imagine your optimistic future and give it faith and trust. If you train yourself that way, you will gain the confidence to trust your imagination more, just like a baby who started out taking clumsy steps end up jogging later in years. That is the force that will cure insomnia.

Life is a continuation of practices. Like a runner that gets up from a fall to run again and again to become a sprinter, you need not become dejected that you cannot find optimistic imaginations. With repeated practice, your imaginations will become robust and using these robust imaginations you will be able to cure insomnia easily.

If thought stays in the present, imagination stays in the future.
If thought makes reality, imagination creates the future.

You should stop your worries about sleep and conjure up optimistic imaginations. Even if you were to die tomorrow, if you continue to be optimistic about tomorrow, you may even be able to evade your fate of death.

8. Medicine for your wounds of insomnia

There is nothing worse than frustration in overcoming insomnia. The reasons for your frustrations may be that you have tried everything and there is no more hope, but these are just your conclusions and they are neither the truths nor the conclusions shared by God.

Just because you cannot find a cure for your insomnia, it doesn't mean that insomnia is an incurable disease. The fact that all your efforts to cure insomnia resulted in failure is no proof that insomnia is incurable – it is proof that your methods were wrong.

Nature is not frustrated or broken in any adversity. Even though there is a forest fire today and all the mountains are left bare, the grasses grow again, the trees grow again, and all the mountains return to their original nature eventually. What nature shows us is the absolute optimism that there can't be frustration in whatever the adversity. We also share such optimism to a certain extent. We don't worry that our heart will stop beating. We don't worry that our lungs will stop breathing. We all share this absolute optimism that our heart and lungs will function indefinitely.

The reason why we have insomnia is that we do not have such optimistic attitude towards sleep. The reason why we don't share the optimism when it comes to sleep is not that we never had such optimism before, but because for some reason we forgot that sleeping itself is a part of life functions comparable to the heart beating and lungs breathing.

If you want to cure insomnia, all you have to do is to recover the absolute optimism on sleep. You need only to recover the memory of absolute optimism. That is to say that such recovery of memory is equal to knowing that all life functions in our body is the same and functions according to the source.

The functions that operate heartbeat, respiration and sleep are the same. They are the same in that they are all controlled by the source. Once you realize this, you become aware that sleep is operated by the same principles as breathing and beating of your heart and how ridiculous it is to worry about sleep.

As all wounds are healed by medicines, the wounds of insomnia also require medicine. But the medicine required is not sleeping pills, special food or teas, exercises and other remedies. The medicine for insomnia is the truth. The truth is that all our life functions are operated by one source!

In addition, the truth that we need not have any worries about these functions. These truths are the real medicines that are required to cure insomnia. Once these medicines are applied to the wounds of insomnia, then the wounds will soon heal, scab will cover the wound and fall off leaving a fresh flesh to replace the wound.

9. The only thing we should fear is fear itself.

Life is always a realm of the unknown. No one knows what will happen in that unknown realm. If you are unlucky, you may die, you may lose all your fortunes, and unexpected misfortunes may fall on you. On the other hand, if you are lucky, unimaginable fortune may fall on you or you may rejoice to find your other half.　You may also become insomniac.

But whatever the case may be, it is foolish to worry about a future that you already concluded to be negative. Even if such unfortunate future may come true, there is nothing to gain by fearing such an outcome other than adding fear to the fear. Therefore, even if the unfortunate event of tomorrow is inevitable, even if the next page of your life has death written in it, you should realize that there is nothing to gain by fearing the inevitable and letting go of your fear of tomorrow will allow you to live your life today without fear.

However, the sleepless night you experienced yesterday will bring you the fear that you will not sleep today and that it will be the same tomorrow. And such fears will inevitably cause insomnia. But you should never be deluded. It was not your insights that predicted insomnia but it was your fear that created it. Therefore, it wasn't that you were insightful but you were foolish. Because you have created insomnia by your fear of it.

Fear is not wisdom for tomorrow. Fear just blocks the vitality of the source with miserable emotional agitation, shrinks me into a poor individual and distorts the normal body's life functions.

If you have insomnia now and you are shivering with fear of it, you must stop adding fear to the fear and believe only that your body universe is in harmony much the same way of the universe. As all universes move through the power of the source and that force works equally in all universes, such belief in the body universe is not absurd or foolish. It is wise, wise, and wise.

You must remember: no matter how hard it is to endure the pain of insomnia, the only thing that you should fear is fear itself. If you are not fearful of fear and remain unaffected by it, you will soon rid yourself of insomnia and normal sleep will eventually find you. That such outcome is as inevitable as morning will come after the night.

10. Insomnia is a blessing

'Insomnia is a blessing. However, insomniacs will never agree with this. 'Insomnia is a blessing?' 'Nonsense!' Of course you are not wrong. If you do not agree that insomnia is a blessing, insomnia is only insomnia and the pain of insomnia is only a pain. But if you agree with it, insomnia is not just insomnia and insomnia can be a blessing for your life and soul.

Insomnia is a great cauldron of fire. In that cauldron of fire, everything you own will melt away. You realize that all your accomplishments, your intellect, and your property are all useless. Your blood boils, your heart torn apart by the continuous pain of insomnia, and you fall into despair knowing that all your possessions are useless in facing insomnia.

But this is only the surface of insomnia. The true nature of insomnia lies within. The true nature of insomnia is the growth of your soul, while on surface only the pain of insomnia appears.

Everyone grows through suffering and the dignity of soul is achieved through pain. Only through pain, can you understand pain, and through pain can you abandon selfishness and egotism, and through pain can you mature the soul to embrace the world.

When you realize the true nature of insomnia by peeling off the surface, you begin to see that beneath the cruel pain of its exterior, lies an enormous opportunity for your soul to mature. In this world where many people, including many discipliners, fall by selfishness and egotism, the chance for you to abandon selfishness and egotism and for your soul to mature through suffering of insomnia can be a great blessing indeed.

Pain and growth always go together. Unhappiness and happiness always go together. It is like two sides of a coin. If you reject one, you cannot obtain the other. If you only accept happiness and reject unhappiness, then it is like living a half of a life without achieving the fullness of one's lives.

If your life has only been comfortable and without grief up until now, if your yesterday was like today and today won't be much different tomorrow, then the arrival of insomnia is a gift of blessing. You will now receive the most desperate pain through insomnia, and through this pain you will finally be free of the cocoon and emerge as a butterfly. Insomnia is such a valuable transformative opportunity.

Insomnia can always be cured. If you believe the

truth and etch it in your heart that the principles of the universe is equal to that of our body, the movement of the universe is equal to that of our body, that the harmony and balance never collapses, and hold these beliefs steadfastly, then insomnia loses strength and will disappear.

If insomnia is a pain that is sure to be cured, if it is not a suffering that ends in pain, if it is an opportunity for our dull souls to become brighter, then the pain from the cauldron of fire of insomnia must not be a mere painful experience but a great blessing for our souls to mature.

11. Sleep functions according to the cosmic law

Sleep comes and goes by cosmic law. It is impossible for humans to control sleeping and waking up. The life functions of the body are the domains of the source, not of man. It is because the source takes care of the work of the life functions that everyone in the world sleeps peacefully every night.

Everyone that sleeps without any problems accepts these principles without even knowing it. Just as you wouldn't hold onto spring and prevent the summer from arriving, these people do not try to control sleep by their will. They merely sleep when sleepy, and wake up when they awake.

However, if you suffer from insomnia, you are trying to go against the flow. You worry that you are unable to sleep and resort to taking sleeping pills and alcohol.

If a person worries that the sky will fall and suffers from the pain of such thoughts, everyone will think he is insane. This is because regardless of this person's beliefs about the sky falling, the fact that the sky will not fall is such an absolute certainty.

But if you have insomnia, you will have similar worries: worried that the sky of sleep will collapse, struggling, suffering and crying because of insomnia, you will do everything you can do to sustain the sky of sleep

That the heaven is up on top and the earth below is a simple cosmic phenomenon. It is also a cosmic phenomenon that we sleep when it is time for sleeping and that we wake up when it is time for waking up. There is no difference between them in that they are cosmic phenomena. Therefore, it is an irony indeed that you should worry that sleep doesn't come and go as you thought it should when you have no such worries about the heaven and earth.

When we intervene in the cosmic phenomenon of sleep, when we worry about the cosmic phenomenon of sleep, just as nature is destroyed with human intervention, the cosmic life functions of the body universe are destroyed. If you know how the sleeping pills you've taken for insomnia has deteriorated your body, then you have to admit this fact.

You should not be dragged by will. Will itself has no boundaries nor good and evil. Will itself is neither ignorant nor wise. Will only acts upon your command. Therefore, it is important that prior to commanding your will, you must first determine whether the command is something that the will is capable of accomplishing and whether the command is right or wrong.

When you reflect on how your body universe works, you naturally come to believe in the existence of your body universe. Your body universe works according to laws of nature. Just as the river flows toward the sea, what you eat and drink is automatically digested. As the sun rises and sets, as the moon rises and sets, your heart works continuously in harmony.

What controls the universe is not your mind. Your will cannot control that. It is the power of the source not you that controls the universe. The only thing you can do is to believe in that power. When you believe in the power of the source, your will cease to worry about not sleeping much like you would not worry about your heart beating.

When we believe in the existence of the source that controls our life functions harmoniously, then calmness and peacefulness of lake replaces the wildfire of worry and anxiety of sleep. Therefore, we need only to believe. The power and intelligence of the source! Nothing else is required, it alone completes life functions.

12. The final resting place of insomnia.

What are your current worries and sufferings? Are there thoughts that refuse to leave your head? If so, you now have a clear choice: Remain in that place or simply leave.

I am sure you want to leave that place as no one wants to remain in such a painful state. But surprisingly, people may elect to stay there. People get so accustomed to anxieties and self-worry, that it becomes harder to leave than to stay. This is how insomniacs tend to opt to remain in that worrisome, painful state rather than leave.

This may be the same for you. If you failed to sleep yesterday and failed to sleep today, your worries and anxiety of today will be bigger than yesterday's worries and anxieties. This means that you never left your anxieties and worries – you remained firmly in them.

You wish to rid yourself of the pain that make you unhappy and leave the worries and anxieties that cause the pain behind but instead end up increasing such worries and anxieties. Such contradicting behaviors stem from ignorance of not knowing what is beneficial for you and what you need to do to remedy the situation.

However, even in such situation you have the option. Whether the choice is for worries and anxieties or the opposite – it is totally up to you. In other words, you have total control to leave your worries and anxieties behind and choose happiness.

Great courage and determination are not necessary to choose happiness over the worries and anxieties. If you have decided to choose happiness over worries and anxieties, your decision to be happy and filling your mind of happy thoughts should be enough.

The power of joy is greater than you think. Instead of filling your mind with worries and anxieties, just having happy thoughts will relieve your stressed nerves and mind, and will lead you to the path away from insomnia.

It is important that you tune yourself to happy thoughts rather than worries and anxieties. You need to make a concerted effort whenever you can.

These happy thoughts will overtake your daily life, having dual effects of ridding yourself from worries and anxieties and returning to bright and positive future, and ridding yourself of insomnia.

You must embrace happiness instead of worries and anxieties. Fall in love – if that is what will ignite your heart. Such passion will overwhelm your thoughts and steer you away from insomnia and there is no better cure.

13. The waves cannot make winds.

Wind can make waves, but waves cannot make winds. This is the basic principle of laws of physics. Mind can make insomnia, but insomnia cannot make the mind. This is a natural principle of the laws of mind.

Insomnia is always caused by the mind. Insomnia is the wave of the mind that the wind of mind creates.

It is impossible to remove the waves from the windy sea. It is also impossible to remove the waves from the windy mind. When the wind calms down, the waves will naturally calm down. When the mind becomes calm, insomnia will be abated.

You should not try to get rid of the wave of insomnia, but instead you have to try to get rid of the wind blowing in mind. The way to get rid of the wind that blows in the mind is to realize that you are the cause of that wind and to stop the delusion of sleep in your mind. The thoughts that you can control sleep, that you can control it through your will, that you have insomnia and cannot be rid of it – these are the winds that are blowing in your mind and the major cause that create the waves of insomnia.

The winds in the mind will cease when you stop these thoughts. Once these thoughts are stopped, peace of mind will follow. Such realization of the cause will make you realize that these winds in the mind are but a figment of your imagination. When you stare straight into something that is not there and realize that it is only an empty vacuum, insomnia cannot exist.

14. Low level healing and the best healing

In the absence of light, darkness is scary and frightening. But as soon as there is light, the darkness disappears and the worry and fear of darkness disappear. Insomnia itself is a form of darkness. Your correct awareness of sleep is the light that will shine on the darkness.

This is the reason why your first response to insomnia should not be to drink milk that was not in your normal diet, to exercise till exhaustion, take medication and other remedies that are said to be good for sleep.

The first thing you must do is to stop all the artificial manipulations and efforts to control the vital functions of sleep, to change your mind to intervene in your sleep and to become aware that falling asleep comes from the power of the source. It is such awareness of sleep which is the light that will eradicate the darkness of insomnia.

Such awareness is possible even in a short time. Time is neither an absolute variable nor a dependent one. Realization that sleep is irrelevant to your thoughts and your will, and that your attempts at manipulating your sleep is futile does not require much time, and such realization can eliminate the darkness of insomnia instantly.

All the remedies you seek such as drinking tea, taking medication and doing exercises, rapt in the idea that you must sleep – all take long time that increase the pain and suffering to the body and mind and are low form of remedies that are total waste of time.

Do not get caught up in the obsession to sleep and

artificial efforts to achieve sleep, and realize through correct awareness of sleep that to be free of insomnia does not take time nor pain or suffering. This is the higher level of remedy that will save you time and unnecessary pain and suffering.

Such experience may sound like a fantasy for people who do not have correct awareness of vital functions, but to those who have such awareness, such experiences are very natural and possible.

15. Understanding instead of avoiding

We all want to avoid suffering. No one likes any kind of suffering

But suffering does not discriminate. There is no mercy or pity in suffering. Suffering does not enjoy our pain, nor does it sympathize with our suffering while driving us to the corner of despair. When such an expressionless and ruthless suffering comes to us, it is only natural for us to fear it and try to avoid it.

But no matter how much you want to avoid suffering, when you realize that you cannot avoid suffering just by your will to avoid it, then the pain becomes bigger due to the sheer apprehension of its inevitability.

Such is the case with people with insomnia. Although they have a strong desire to free themselves from insomnia, their pain grow stronger with the realization that they cannot solve the problem through their own will alone. Such is the dilemma with the people suffering from insomnia.

If you too are suffering from this dilemma of wanting to escape insomnia but instead falling deeper into it, it is your passive attitude to avoid the pains associated with insomnia rather than to cope with insomnia wisely that keeps you in such dilemma.

Regardless of the subject matter, if your reaction is to psychologically block out the problem without an objective analysis of the problem, then the pain will expand indefinitely.

There are many insomniacs who suffer from delusions that their conditions will end their lives and that the suffering is so great that it would be better to die. For the most part, the suffering these people experience is not from the physical pain of insomnia itself, but from made up pain that is nonexistent.

Whether it's insomnia, college entrance examination, success in business – fear is present in everyday endeavors. Fear of failure, illness and rejection – but if you do not feed these fears with unsubstantiated concerns, in surprisingly most instances, the problems tend to solve themselves out or dissipated.

When you want to reduce or eliminate the pain caused by an object, passive avoidance is always the worst solution.

If you suffer from insomnia, confronting the problem instead of avoidance is the best solution.

Once you confront the pain, understand the pain, and correctly identify the cause of the pain, then the path to cope and to escape the pain will become visible, which you could not see when you were too busy trying to avoid the pain.

16. Calming the storm of the mind

No one wants to sail the stormy seas for fear of being swept away to die. So when there is a storm, fishermen moor their boats to the harbor and those who work or play on the beach hastily take shelter away from the beach. Even if no one tells them to do so, people instinctively know that it is wise to take shelter and that it would be foolish to ignore the warnings.

Such physical storms also exist in the mind. The storms within the mind take the form of agony, conflict, anger, fear, anxiety and worries. And if you have insomnia, such storms can grow to be category 5 storms.

Many people succumb to the storm of the mind created by insomnia, ultimately losing everything in the process. However, what they don't realize is that it wasn't insomnia but themselves that led to such a loss. Insomniacs invariably create the storm of the mind themselves and then struggle and suffer from the storm.

The problem with the storms of the mind is that it is very difficult to realize that the storm was created by me and can also be solved by me. Worries beget more worries, anxieties beget more anxieties, but rarely the cause of worries and anxieties are identified.

That is why it may be easy to create the storm but hard to escape it. Anxiety and fear are easier to create than to erase. Once the storm is created it is difficult to rid of it and grow stronger as you try harder to get rid of it.

Insomniacs are the prime example. When sleep deprivation continues, worry, anxiety and fear are created in the mind which cannot be escaped. But all that anxiety, worry and fear are merely the storm of mind that they created.

The storm of the mind can easily be resolved by oneself. However scared and worried about insomnia, once you realize that it is only an illusion created in your mind, and as long as you hold onto that realization wholeheartedly, the storm will subside and dissipate itself.

17. Most effective action for healing insomnia.

An action is required in order to achieve a result. Efforts are required to achieve success, courtship is needed for love and exercises are required to gain health.

If these represent visible actions, there are also some invisible actions – they are actions of thoughts and emotions. And in the case of insomnia, these invisible actions are far more important than the visible ones. Taking medications, eating foods, exercising, and basking in the sun, does not do much to cure your insomnia.

It is only ignorance and delusion that insomnia will be cured through these visible actions. In fact, few people have been healed of their insomnia through such a way.

The way to cure insomnia isn't through visible actions but through invisible actions that are decisive for curing insomnia. In other words, your thoughts and emotions about insomnia are the keys to solving your insomnia.

Sleep is a picture drawn on the canvas of the mind by the paints of thoughts and emotions. So, if you have uneasy thoughts and feelings about sleep, you are already painting a picture of insomnia on the canvas of your mind and that is why insomnia cannot be easily erased.

On the contrary, if you have an optimistic attitude towards sleep: 'I did not sleep yesterday, but every day is different.' 'If there is a downhill, there is also an uphill.' 'All things have an end and so does Insomnia.' If you draw the pictures of these thoughts and emotions in your mind, you have taken the steps out of insomnia and are taking the actions out of insomnia.

The visible actions such as taking medication, exercising exhaustively and listening to soft music are very crude and unrefined approaches. Instead of searching for outside help, there is a far more effective and decisive action. That is to find optimistic thoughts and feelings of sleep within your mind. There is no better remedy for insomnia.

18. Insomnia is Murphy's Law?

No matter how much you want to sleep, no matter how sleepy you are, no matter how hard you try to get out of insomnia, when you cannot sleep you think of Murphy's law: 'Everything that can go wrong, will go wrong.' But that is a mistake. The reason why you cannot achieve good results is not because your fate is predetermined, but because your mind, or the center of gravity of your thoughts, is tilted towards bad outcome.

Insomnia has the tendency to follow your mindset. Although in the exterior you pursue happiness but in your mind you are afraid of bad results, then the center of gravity of your thoughts is tilted towards misfortune and the unfortunate outcome cannot be avoided.

You may protest: 'I have more positive thoughts

than negative ones. I have not much worry about sleep. I just cannot sleep.' But there is no such a thing. It does not matter that the positive thoughts are 99% and the negative thought is 1%.

The important thing is the density of thought, not the volume. If the anxiety and the fear of insomnia exist in the corner of your mind no one knows about, then 99% of your positive thoughts may be only superficial and 1% of your negative thoughts could be fundamental and it is only natural that you cannot escape insomnia.

Insomnia does not follow Murphy's Law. Insomnia just follows the center of gravity of your mind. Where is the center of gravity of your mind? Knowing that is the key to solving insomnia.

19. Change your subconscious

No matter how much you want to avoid it, no matter how hard you try, you tell yourself that you shouldn't do this and that you should stop, if the anxiety and fear of insomnia creep in, it means you have become a slave to your subconscious.

Subconscious follows the thoughts and emotions you put into your mind. If you've experienced extreme anxiety and panic attack, such fears and anxiety will creep into your subconscious and will dominate it.

In other words, no matter how much you try to avoid the fear and anxiety, when you encounter situations similar to the events that your subconscious had been created in the first place, invariably your subconscious will be triggered to dominate your consciousness not to be afraid and anxious with fear and anxiety.

There is no right or wrong in subconscious. There is no truth or falsehood in subconscious. Just having repeated thoughts and intense emotions about a subject, your subconscious will accept it as truth and regurgitate as reality regardless of right and wrong.

It is not your consciousness but your subconscious that governs you. When your subconscious has been entrenched in negative thoughts, occasional positive thoughts are not enough to stop your subconscious to take over your reality.

If you want to change your reality, you have to change your subconscious. If you want to get out of your insomnia, you have only to change your subconscious.

The way to change the subconscious mind is to have more intense thoughts and feelings than the thoughts and emotions that went into creating the past subconscious. Whatever the state of your current insomnia, more intense, persistent, steadfast optimism and positive thinking on sleep will eventually seep into your subconscious and change it.

The subconscious has the ability to change the impossible to the possible. It has the ability to make you cross a terrifying wooden bridge effortlessly that you would never have crossed using only your consciousness. What seemed like Mount Everest until yesterday can seem like a little hill today.

20. Mind for healing and Mind for learning

People with insomnia often say that they find themselves unable to sleep one day. But when I look into them closely, they always have some reasons. The most distinctive feature is that the true self has chosen insomnia as a lesson for our growth.

The true self does not care if one is rich or poor nor the social status – it is only concerned about the growth of its existence.

We don't learn through happiness. We always learn and grow through suffering. When we suffer from sickness, failure, sadness and pain, only then do we get up from the idleness of happy days and make efforts to cope with the suffering and gain insights and grow.

The suffering from insomnia also has the same

purpose. Therefore, just trying to avoid the pain of insomnia always has its limitations. If we only try to avoid the pain, then we cannot gain the growth of our true self by carefully looking into our inner mind and therefore the cure for insomnia is that much harder to attain.

A deep understanding of the mind and being is a necessary precondition for healing insomnia. Those who study this will be able to rid insomnia one day without even realizing. Once you learn the true nature of the existence and because such learning has altered the state of existence, insomnia has completed its mission and will disappear.

People suffering from illness rarely go on with life without studying their illness. They study about their illness because they try desperately to rid themselves of the illness. The same is true of insomniacs.

As such, the need to learn follows the need for cure and much like birds needing two wings to fly, these needs are like the two wings that are needed to fly to the freedom from insomnia.

21. Insight or repetition

It is difficult to escape from insomnia just by wanting to escape from it. The idea of sleep should be dramatically changed in order to escape insomnia. There are two methods. One is an intuitive insight into the life principle. Another is a repeated awareness of this principle.

Intuitive insight changes sleep in a short period of time. The instant you gain an insight into the life principle, insomnia disappears in that instant. It is similar to Shantideva's words that no matter how great and grave the sin committed, it can be erased the instant you attain compassion.

Repetitive awareness changes sleep over a long period of time. Awareness of the life principle is weak at first, but as you repeatedly engrave it into your mind, your awareness gets deeper and deeper, and your insomnia disappears at some point. It is as if the thick dust that is accumulated can be finally removed by continuous mopping.

There is no difference between the two in that they change sleep. They are neither superior nor inferior in changing sleep. The only difference is in their methods. And perhaps they are equal in that respect. Repetitive awareness is transformed into intuitive insight and intuitive insight grows into repetitive awareness. Like flowers and fruit, they are of one body.

Intuitive insights into and repeated awareness of the life principle – these are the key elements to healing insomnia that cannot be ignored. One of these elements must be obtained.

22. Right Understanding and Attitude toward Stress

Stress is the psychological friction that arises from not understanding myself, not understanding others (world or reality) and failing to understand the conflicts that arise between me and others.

Why am I in this situation? Why should I suffer from this pain? Why should I be treated like this? Why should I experience this injustice, etc. When I find it difficult to understand so many "whys", stress is increased or decreased according to the gravity of these whys.

This is the same with insomnia. Why did I get insomnia? Why do I have to go through life with insomnia? ...... Like many thoughts of "why me", when the current situation cannot be explained and can't figure out how to relieve these questions, then the stress of sleep increase and insomnia gets worse.

But whether that is stress, insomnia or anything else, these are all aspects of the cycle of happiness and unhappiness. Life inevitably contains cycles of happiness and unhappiness and they repeat in life without a pattern. If there are good times, there are bad times – like the changing of the seasons.

Just as no one can avoid the change of seasons, the happiness and unhappiness of life cannot be avoided. As spring, summer, autumn and winter come and go according to the law of nature, the happiness and unhappiness of life that turns around life is a law of life that nobody can avoid.

Therefore, if you encounter hard and painful times against your will, it means that you have come to the winter of your life according to the happiness and unhappiness cycle of life.

What is important then is the mental attitude of moderation. That is to say that when spring of life cycle arrives, it is important to realize that this is not permanent, be thankful for your good fortunes and to share such happiness without being intoxicated in it.

That is how when the winter of life arrives you do not lose hope and courage wrapped in despair, with the realization that this too is not permanent and that spring will come again. This mental attitude of moderation will help you to overcome the stress during the winter cycle of your life.

Just as winter is not a subject to be liked or disliked, stress cannot be avoided and is but a process of growing pains that one must overcome in the course of one's life.

If we do not have any stress in life, if we do not have any failures and frustrations, if we succeed in everything we do without any real effort and patience, then there will be little joy in seeing the light out of the darkness. We will have no joy to escape unhappiness and enjoy happiness.

Therefore, stress is necessary part of life. It is an indispensable menu in the dining table of life. No matter how delicious, it is not fun to eat only one menu all the time. In fact, it would not be just boring but unhealthy. Do you have various stresses? Well then, you are now given a new opportunity to widen your menu of life for a healthier and more mature soul.

Stress is your chance for your soul to take a leap. All you have to do is to accept your life's homework that is stress with open heart, just as you would accept the changes of the seasons.

Your attitude should not be "this is not what I want". Instead, "such is life", "this too will end" and "there must be light at the end of the tunnel" are the proper attitudes that will let you weather the different seasons of life.

When you open your mind to stress this way, the stress that seemed like the seed of unhappiness will turn into the seed of happiness overnight. When you face stress in such a different light, stress may disappear overnight.

This is the nature of the universe (mind). The moment you open your mind to pain, your soul grows naturally in the process of fighting and resisting the pain. The moment you accept pain, the need for pain disappears – there no longer exist the requirement for pain.

If all you did was think one open thought but your

insomnia disappears overnight, that means that open thought did the homework of having to go through pain for you. That one open thought has made the existence of insomnia insignificant, requisite in your growth that the universe has endowed upon you.

When the work is done, the task disappears, much like seasons move on after its time is due. The pain of insomnia will disappear automatically once its task is accomplished.

23. You should not make contradictory demands.

Hypochondriacs think they are always sick. Healthy people do not dwell on the sickness. This is the difference between a hypochondriac and a healthy person.

Insomniacs always have sleep on their minds. Healthy people do not. This is the difference between an insomniac and a normal person.

Intelligent people will have noticed a correlation. Yes! Body and mind are interrelated and the state of the mind is projected directly into the body. Peace of mind will bring comfort to the body while unstable mind will make your body uneasy. If your mind is suffering from the fear and anxiety from insomnia, your body will reflect this state of the mind and comfortable sleep will become unattainable.

Most insomniacs miss this correlation. They forget that the mind and the body are interrelated and wish the body to be comfortable even though the mind is uneasy. They wish for a comfortable sleep while their minds are filled with fear and anxiety about sleep. Just as it is futile to wish for sunlight during rainstorm and to wish for spring in winter, such contradictory demands cannot be realized.

If the mind is calm, so is the body. If the mind is calm, sleep comes naturally.

If you really want to sleep, you should cease these contradictory demands for normal sleep when your mind is filled with fear and anxiety. Such demands are but a pipe dream.

24. There is a path in the cause

Insomnia is a like a dark cave. The way out of the dark cave is neither to adapt to the cave nor to wander the cave aimlessly. The only escape from the cave is to figure out the exit and to follow the path to the exit.

However, much of the people in the cave of insomnia wander aimlessly within the cave, take medication to calm the anxiety. Such actions are not helpful in figuring out the way out of the cave, but to cope with the environment of the cave. The way out of this cave is to figure out the reason for going into the cave in the first place, not to adapt to its environment.

If you suffer insomnia, you should stop trying to get rid of insomnia thoughtlessly and try to find out the cause of insomnia. And once you realize that the cause of your insomnia is in the mind, you will realize how futile medicines and foods are to curing insomnia.

Then, you get to stop these useless acts and stop being obsessed with sleep and watch sleep eventually and naturally come with the flow of nature. It is then that you will find calm in your mind. Once your mind finds the calm then your body will also find calm and sleep will find its way home.

Finding the cause of insomnia is the only way out of its cave. This is the truth not only in insomnia but in most other matters.

25. Insomnia is but a figment of your imagination

Insomnia is but a figment of your imagination. Insomniacs find out about their symptoms and struggle with insomnia, but they are only imprisoning themselves in the prison of their making. The fact that you are instantly freed from that insomnia that painfully kept you awake up until yesterday and suddenly return to your normal sleep as soon as you realize your insomnia is gone proves the point.

There is no fixed substance in the mind. But as soon as you think random night that you couldn't sleep as a fixed substance, a prison of insomnia is created and you are trapped in it. No matter how much you cry out in it, to the universe (God) you are just pitiful. You are only stuck in a prison created in the figment of your imagination.

The reality of insomnia you are struggling with is but a figment of your imagination. The only reason for the existence of insomnia is because you think it exists. As soon as you realize this, insomnia will disappear.

Realizing that nothing is there and fighting against nothing is just a futile effort and that such futility is but a comedy of errors is the right path to cure and the most effective way to rid yourself of insomnia.

26. When spring blooms in the heart

Winter is a cold and freezing season. However, no matter how thick the ice frozen, the ice that had no signs of thawing in manmade bonfires, has no chance against slow warming of spring sunshine.

If you are suffering the pains of insomnia, your heart is in the middle of winter. If the pain of insomnia has been long, the winter of your heart was as long and the ice of your heart is as thick. To melt such thick ice, no amount of paper and logs you burn will be sufficient to melt that ice. The best thing to do is to bring spring into your heart to melt that thick ice.

The way to bring spring to your heart is not to try to control your sleep with your thoughts, but to believe in the complete vital function of sleep itself.

You believed in the complete vital function of sleep itself when you did not suffer insomnia. You had no worry or anxiety about sleep. Your heart believed in the vital function of sleep. You must restore that heart now.

What you need to do now is not to look for medicine that will cure insomnia, but to have your awareness and belief in the source that you had from birth that governs the vital functions of sleep.

The signal of the spring that melts your thickly frozen heart is a firm faith and trust in the source that grows in your heart. When you really believe it, your heart becomes comfortable of itself. Your sleep also gets better by itself. The pain of insomnia will end.

27. Awareness is a pathway to a new world

Your awareness of something new opens the door to a new world from the old and poor thought. If you need a change and want to make that change a way out, you need to open your eyes to a new and fresh awareness away from the thoughts that you are trapped in now.

It is more so if you suffer insomnia. No matter how much you know about insomnia, if such knowledge does not help you with insomnia, you must abandon the obsolete and useless knowledge and find a new and practical awareness that will free you from that suffering.

A new and true awareness of sleep is the awareness that sleep is a vital function of the source and that it is a process that happens by itself according to the principle of vital function, not the object of thought and will. This is a new and true awareness of sleep.

Therefore, if you are sleepy, you will fall asleep. If you are not sleepy, you will not fall asleep. There is no problem in itself. So, if you had tried to have some influence on sleep and had wanted to control sleep according to your desire because you could not fall asleep, you should know that this is the main cause of insomnia. If you had tried to heal insomnia by various remedies such as drinking milk, seeing sunshine, exercising, taking half-baths, consuming food that are supposed to be good for sleep, etc, that you have tried countless times before, then you should know that those efforts have been the main culprits of insomnia.

This is comparable to being obsessed with catching a few lowly soldiers instead of capturing the enemy's general. You cannot win the war by catching a few lowly soldiers. You must capture the enemy's general. That is the way to end the war.

Trivial and tiring fights with lowly soldiers is a time consuming way of wasting energy, but capturing the enemy's general will be a critical stroke of blow that can win the war quickly and effectively.

A new and true awareness of sleep is quick solution to relieving the pain of insomnia. It is like quick end to a war through capturing the enemy's general.

What is the mind that is formed through new and true awareness of sleep? It is a mind which has no doubts about what the source does. It is a mind that has no reservations about the leap of faith. If you have such a mind about sleep, insomnia will fade away much like the darkness retreats with the crack of dawn.

28. The Importance of Confidence

Confidence is trust in myself. There is no better medicine than this. In a way, your search for good medicine, good hospital, and for good doctors, are all a process in finding this confidence. Your struggle to escape from your desperate situation is your desperate search to find the confidence required to survive.

If your thoughts are swayed by the varied possibilities and lack confidence, your mind is inevitably unstable and anxious. Such mind creates insomnia and when connected with nerves, it creates neurosis such as obsessional neurosis, depression, manic depression. All the above symptoms are created due to lack of confidence.

The secret to having confidence is the truth. When you know the truth, it becomes faith. When you know the truth, it itself becomes confidence. There is no greater confidence than knowing the truth.

What is the truth to get out of insomnia? It is that the power of the source will take care of the vital functions of body in perfect harmony. It is that the force of the source will make your sleep come and go in perfect harmony by itself.

There is no need to place any doubts on this. One look at your vital functions and such doubts become irrelevant. Your vital functions are not governed by your will. You breathe regardless of your thoughts and your heart beats without any control from your mind. If you look at these vital functions, you come to the conclusion that some unknown power takes care of your body without your control and that your sleep is also a part of this vital function. With that awareness, insomnia automatically disappears.

29. You heal as much as you desire.

Everything in the world follows its own path in nature. Rocks, trees, flowers, grass, rain, wind, etc, all exist and follow their paths in nature. Flowers do not bloom randomly and out of the blue. Flowers are never lazy or indolent in following its nature to thrive and to bloom.

Flowers reveal the essence of existence by their best efforts at blooming. This is not unique to flowers. From the trees that grow deep in the mountains to lowly weeds that grow regardless of people's desires for their existence, all follow and grow their paths in nature.

Everything that surrounds us exists in its own nature. There is sincerity, an indomitable will and an absolute positive mind and desperation.

It is not just a simple biological process that spring buds bloom through hardened surface of the land. There is an existential desperation of sustaining life. Flowers bloom in the last stage of their lifecycle. The flowers that bloom are the ultimate manifestation of their desperate survival.

Desperation to achieve maturity is the hidden motivation of all things in the world. Flowers, weeds, rain, and winds, all have their desperate agenda and in this desperate harmony do we find true nature's beauty.

Just as all things exist through their desperation, so should the people with insomnia. Desperation is not an obsession. It is a sincere plea without prejudice. It is an act of sincerity

The reason challenging insomnia is cured by a single word of truth is because true thoughts and actions can break through the frozen minds of insomniacs.

The important thing is your daily attitude. This is because your daily attitude does not only apply merely to daily things but also in all your affairs. If you approach your everyday life with desperation and sincerity in everything you do, you can overcome any difficulty. But if you lack this desperation and handle your affairs halfheartedly, such attitude will make it harder for you to escape insomnia.

However, insomnia is sure to be cured. In order for you to achieve this truth, you need to be desperate.

When you are truly desperate, the answer comes out from within. When you are truly desperate, your eyes will see the solution. Desperation is the key to moving the heavens and solving the problem.

30. Hatred and aversion also cause insomnia.

Hatred and aversion towards others can also cause insomnia. When you hate someone, hate his presence, hate to face him, despise him, uncomfortable to be around and feel displeasure to be with him, and always reminded of the bad things he did to you, such recurring thoughts can cause insomnia. Unfiltered and violent feelings such as hatred and aversion can create tensions in the body, interfere with sleep required in the relaxed state and cause insomnia.

The best way to get rid of such feelings is to turn them into compassion. "I hate him, I hate to be with him, I hate to talk to him, I hate to be with him under the same sky ... ..." Do not increase the hatred in such thoughts. "Everyone has shortcomings. He is not evil, but just lacking. He is lacking in thought, lacking in consideration for others – A lot of traits that I once shared. "This is how you change your mind.

The truth is, every hatred and aversion stems from our lack of knowledge and understanding of others. Misunderstanding the language and actions of others can create and fuel the hatred and anger in the mind.

Once you decide to understand and forgive, your hatred and aversion turns into a sense of compassion. And once such compassion creeps in, your hatred and aversion calm the emotional wave of hatred and aversion and the waves of hatred and aversion that caused the insomnia will subside.

31. You cannot enter a good university without studying hard

Many people suffering from lack of sleep are worried because sleeping is that much important. Even in this day and age where food, clothing and shelter are so abundant, if you are suffering from insomnia, everything becomes meaningless.

This is why insomniacs try so hard to overcome insomnia. They eat and exercise regularly and do whatever it is required to do. But still find it hard to overcome insomnia. This is like cramming for exams for totally unrelated subject. If you study for English when the exam is for math, no matter how hard you study, your efforts will be in vain.

Insomnia is the same. No matter how hard you try, it would not be helpful for the cure of insomnia if you do not tackle the core of the problem, much like cramming for an exam that is unrelated to the subject.

Just as you have to study wisely in learning the core of the problems that will likely appear in the entrance exams to a good university, in order to solve the problem of insomnia, you must learn the core of the problem of insomnia.

What is the core of the problem of insomnia? The core problem of insomnia refers not to random knowledge of sleep, but to wise knowledge of the vital functions of the body, tenacious and steadfast quest for knowledge for correct awareness.

This requires that you study the vital functions of your body, and that you should study tenaciously, steadfastly without hesitation and to retain your correct awareness of the life principle.

If you have insomnia and need to solve the

problem, you should not miss the core of the life principle like a student who does not miss the core of learning. If you follow the core of the life principle in the beginning and slack off after a while, it will be difficult to cure insomnia. Much like nonchalant halfhearted studying will not get you through the doors of top universities, halfhearted and nonchalant knowledge of the life principle will not allow you to escape insomnia.

32. Empathize with the Truth

The best way to grow flowers is not to be infatuated with the blooming but to do your best in watering it. In order to escape insomnia, it will not be your infatuation with sleep but your best efforts in understanding the life principle that will rescue you from insomnia.

Nurturing cannot be hastened. Haste does not make flowers bloom faster, nor does it make insomnia disappear faster. There are no quick ways for flowers to bloom. Insomnia also cannot be hastened. Much like flowers can die while you try to prompt it to bloom too early, your haste to cure yourself of insomnia may actually harm the process.

If sufficient water and sunlight is provided, the flower will bloom naturally. Studying the life principle and if the studying matures in the mind, insomnia will disappear and natural sleep will come to you.

Such efforts does not require much time, efforts or sweat. It only requires that you realize the truth. Then one day you will say to yourself "That's right" and the realization of truth will be in your grasp.

A person who recovered from insomnia in just two days sent me this message: "I did not know yesterday, but I know today!" This is the empathy with truth. Knowing something today which I did not know yesterday. Such a moment of realization, that is empathy. That person was cured of insomnia by that empathy.

33. Love that can overcome insomnia

Every living thing consummates perfect bond through love. Humans also achieve perfect bond through love. There is no better medium than love when it comes to consummating. Love is a perfectly ideal medium for consummation.

The normal vital function of our body is the proof that there is such love between me and the source. The fact that my heart beats normally and that I breathe normally is a testimony of such love.

Alternatively, the fact that I have insomnia is a proof that there is no love between me and the source. Instead of entrusting myself to the power of the source, the fact that I am relying on alcohol, medicine and other methods to influence the worries and anxieties of insomnia is also an indication of this lost love.

If you want to return to normal sleep, your job is too simple. That is to love the source deeply. That is to infinitely trust in the vital function of the source. That is to believe that sleep is also a harmonious work of the source, as the source makes the heart beat perfectly and harmonizes breathing. In such love and faith, insomnia naturally becomes normal sleep.

When you love something so deeply more than your life, you can obtain and grasp whatever you want. When you love the source so deeply more than your life, The sleep you want so desperately can be obtained. Love in moderation cannot get your true love.

34. Will is poison in overcoming Insomnia

The will power always affects our thoughts, feelings and actions. Our will power is indispensable for of our lives. No matter how small of big the decision, our will power is involved in those decisions.

Will power is the power exerted when our will to act on some action is added with the energy. If we were to decide to do a bad deed, our will power will make that deed possible. Likewise, if we decide to do some good deeds, then our will power will also make that deed possible.

As such, will is only a means of self-realization and there is no good or bad in itself. But using will to overcome insomnia is like taking poison.

The relationship between sleep and will is equivalent to water and fire. Sleep happens when our will is absent and our will can only be activated when we are awake.

Taking sleeping pills in order to sleep, consuming food in order to sleep, drinking tea in order to sleep, taking acupuncture in order to sleep, taking Chinese medicine in order to sleep, etc. All these actions with "in order to sleep" motivations have been exercised by our will.

Therefore, all these actions taken by our will power in order to sleep have the opposite effect. It should be obvious that all these actions taken "in order to sleep" by our will power is not going to make us sleep. How can we expect to fall asleep while trying to wake up at the same time?

If sleep is a flowing river, you are a boat on that river. The ship should follow the flow of the river. The ship cannot flow upstream. When will power is exercised, you are trying to go against the flow of the river. Such attempts will never succeed, and will only leave you exhausted.

If you want to sleep, you should let go of your will to sleep and ride the natural flow of life like a ship that flows down the river. Just letting go of your will to sleep will allow your symptoms of insomnia to float down the river into normal sleep.

35. Night goes, and dawn comes

There are two ways in which people see the world. One sees the world with its brains while the other by heart. The insomniacs are the former.

Those that see the world with their brains try to squeeze their knowledge in order to beat insomnia, and when all ideas have been exhausted they fall into despair and confusion. Having exhausted all methods in their disposal, the brain cannot come up with better ideas to beat insomnia.

But this isn't because insomnia is an incurable disease – it wasn't curable because the problem cannot be solved by the brain. If sleep is governed by the brain, then you should fall asleep as soon as your brain commands it. However, that never happens and no matter how much you command the sleep to be activated and that is because sleep doesn't respond to your commands.

Sleep is governed by existence. Sleep is governed by heart. To resolve insomnia, you have to use your heart instead of the brain. The journey from head to heart is a journey from thought to feeling.

Therefore, insomniacs must stop interfering sleep with thoughts and start experiencing their vital functions with the heart. Embracing sleep by heart is very similar to true love shared by a man and a woman. The sheer happiness experienced just by the thought of each other should be the same experience shared by the heart and sleep.

Even when sleep evades us, even when our thoughts tell us that sleep won't be coming, just as our existence will do what our existence needs to do, just as the roots will do whatever is necessary for the leaves to survive, if our heart truly believes that the source will do whatever is necessary for the sleep to appear, then my life function will do its job. Sleep will appear on its own, just as full moon begets crescent moon, and clouds will be cleared by the winds.

36. The problem itself is not a problem

"Can I escape from insomnia?" When I meet people who have been suffering from insomnia for a long time, they all ask me this. But the conclusion is simple. No matter how bad your condition is, you can escape insomnia.

Your problem is that you just do not know the way. Since you've had insomnia, you've lost yourself. Like shaking reeds, like rolling leaves, shaking weakly even in small worries instead of dreaming of hopes of life, accepting everything with desolation and desperation, you feel the survival itself is a huge wall.

But there is no insomnia which you cannot escape from. The fact that you have had insomnia for a long time isn't because you cannot get out of insomnia, but it is because you are just lost.

Since insomnia occurs inside you, you must find the solution from within. Inner solutions do not include taking medication and food or exercising. The only way to resolve your insomnia is to stop looking for solutions outside, but to go inside you and to contemplate thusly: Why do I have insomnia now? What is the cause of the problem? What to do and how to do it......

If you go inside you and look at yourself, you will see that what you have done outside your mind is not the way to solve insomnia. You can see that insomnia does not disappear from taking medicines, exercising and listening to music. And you finally realize that sleep does not need such artificial attempts or manipulations. If this awareness occurs within you, your insomnia will get better. This improvement of insomnia results from your right awareness and attitude toward

insomnia.

The problems of life are always not the problems themselves, but our attitude toward the problems. Since the problems of life are themselves our growth engines, the problems themselves cannot be problems. If there were no problems in life and every moment was smooth sailing, wouldn't we all become pathetic egomaniacs with no chance of learning patience, humility, enlightenment, and wisdom?

Therefore, your insomnia is not a problem at all. All your attempts to overcome insomnia, even your struggle to find the solution outside are good experiences and by overcoming these failed attempts at finding the solution will bring new insights and attitudes that will guide you through life. Therefore, you need not complain or grumble for having insomnia. For you will surely gain the rewards comparable to the pain you have suffered.

37. Peace and calm is your original form.

If you have insomnia, it is because your mind has worries and anxieties, there will not be calm and peace of mind, and you may come to believe that the psychological agitations like worry, anxiety, and fear that occupy your mind is your real existence. Since you have had insomnia, it is only natural for you to think of the psychological atrophy and agitation which have never left you yesterday, a month ago, a year ago, and the decades ago as your reality.

But that's not real you. The psychological oppression and agitation suffered by insomnia, your suffering and pain resulting from such results are your image reflected in the mirror of your distorted mind and is not your true existence and does not reflect what is inherent in you and exists eternally.

Your true existence is calm and peace. Just as you cannot deny that the sky is blue no matter how cloudy rainy and windy it may be, any hardship that comes to you will never destroy or break calm and peace in you. This is because you are essentially a cosmos, and harmony, calm, and peace that are the attributes of cosmos are your own attributes.

Therefore, losing your original existence of calm and peace due to the pain and fear from insomnia, and thinking of anxiety and fear as fate are nothing more than foolish, pathetic and disgusting self-pity and self-deceit similar to the ignorant belief that the color of cloud is the color of sky.

No matter how difficult and painful you feel now, no matter how endless anxiety and fear surround you, it is only an imagination that passes through your head and is not your original image that you were born with.

You have always slept quietly and peacefully in your childhood. The times when you slept as soon as your head hit the pillow is not just an image you conjured up but your true essence that you were born with.

Therefore, the fact that you have insomnia now and are so distressed by it, is only in your mind that is suffering from momentary confusion. What you need to do to get back to normal sleep is a realization that your thoughts filled with worries and anxieties of sleep are just an illusion. That realization will awake your sleeping soul and show you your true essence.

You are a universe, harmony, calm and peace. The moment you realize that you are such a universe, the moment you realize that your essence is universe of harmony and peace, you know that all the worries, anxieties, and fears made by insomnia are transitory clouds, not eternal sky.

When we know that the sky is always blue sky, the clouds no longer become sky.

When we know that we are the cosmos, when we know that we are a perfect cosmic vital function, insomnia made by illusion does not dominate us anymore.

38. The way to live and the way to die

No one in the world wants to die. Even the people who want to die, they actually want to live. Even if they desire to die because life is too difficult and would rather choose death, at the moment of truth they feel desperate hope for life.

The same is true for people suffering insomnia. Even if they suffer insomnia and would rather die due to extreme anxiety and fear, all the people that I met were struggling to live: they go to hospitals, go to Chinese medicine clinics, take pills, bask in the sun, listen to music, exercise, consume food that are supposed to be good for sleep. However, they never realized that these actions for survival are the very thing that will kill them.

The moment a mind is desperately searching for the way to live, the way that is led by the death of your mind becomes no longer visible. The moment the mind eagerly searches for ways to sleep, you realize sleep where the mind must die does not exist. The mind will not rest in finding a road to survival and there is no peaceful sleep where the mind does not rest.

Sleep only comes when the mind is at rest. When your worries and anxieties about sleep are resting, when your thirst and desires for resolving insomnia are finally laid to rest, that is the moment when you can finally fall asleep.

However, it is not as easy for those with strong wills. Perhaps for these people their will power is more important than the truth about the healing of insomnia. Despite all the suffering they endured due to insomnia, they consider their thoughts more important than the truth that makes them escape from insomnia. Although they accept the truth of the life principle, as soon as insomnia kicks in, they go back to their old habit of thinking: "I have to sleep to order to live ... ..." "I have to sleep to get to work tomorrow ... ..." "I'm afraid I will not be able to sleep like this ... ..."

The mind to live, that is, the mind to sleep, makes you obsessed with sleep and does not solve insomnia. Everyone who sleeps well without any problems has no such obsessions with sleep. Even if he does not sleep well, he does not feel nervous. He only falls asleep when he is sleepy. Whether he sleeps well or not, the mind does not cling to sleep.

However, people with problems with sleep always cling to sleep and worry about sleep. They are worried that they cannot sleep when they cannot sleep and are worried that they sleep when they sleep: they are worried that they will not be able to sleep well tomorrow because they could not sleep well today and they are worried they will not sleep well tomorrow even if they slept well today. If your mind is preoccupied with such worries and if your insomnia is still not healed, you would be right in thinking that the culprit is your mind struggling desperately to sleep in order to survive.

The mind clinging to your sleep is the way to die. To free your mind of these thoughts is the way to live. Even when you cannot sleep, you should believe: Just as the seasons rotate according to the natural cycle, sleeping and waking up will eventually return to its natural order.

Nature is not representative of the things that are in front of you. Just as spring, summer, winter and fall rotate according to the cycle of nature, your body and your sleep not returning to their the natural cycle is not possible.

You should always reflect on your thoughts and actions. You should determine whether it is way to live or way to die. That determination is simple and easy. If you are obsessed with sleep and worried about sleep, you are on your way to die. If you forsake your obsession with sleep, you are on your way to live.

39. Wisdom not to do what you shouldn't do

The common characteristic shared by the people suffering from insomnia is that they struggle to fall asleep. They all try things that are said to be good for sleep, go to hospitals, take sleeping pills and basically anything and everything they possibly can.

However, these attempts almost always end in failure, and despite those failures they continue to repeat the same mistakes without realizing why and fall into deeper desperation. They feel despair and even think that their life is over because they have done all their best to sleep, but failed to do it.

There is a common mistake with these people. It is that they do what they should not do. If you do what you should not do for sleep, your sleep cannot get better no matter how hard you try. If you have a problem, you have to solve it and try to find a solution, but if you keep doing things that you should not do, it's like digging your own grave.

If you have a problem with sleep and you have to solve this problem, at least you have to have wisdom not to do the things that you should not do, such as not taking sleeping pills, stop thinking insomnia as a problem of your mind but as a problem of your body, not bothering your body with medical examinations and stop the useless worries and anxieties, and so on. If it is difficult to stop these things all at once, then try to stop them one by one starting with the easiest thing for you.

It may seem trivial, but simple things such as quitting things that you shouldn't do that disrupt your sleep alone can prevent further damage of insomnia and improve your conditions that can lead to the cure of insomnia.

40. Always benefit yourself

The most common mistake made by insomniacs is that they don't do the things that are beneficial to them. What these people are good at is doing the things that are harmful to them.

As soon as their sleep weren't to their satisfaction, any remnants of positive thoughts go out the window and instead are filled with negative thoughts such as anxiety and fear. And if their sleep disorders persist, they bask in the correctness of their foresight while falling deeper in the pitfalls of insomnia.

The irony of gloating in the pool of their premonition of insomnia while falling deeper in the pitfalls of insomnia is a common recurring pattern for insomniacs.

This tendency to fill their minds with negative

thoughts by insomniacs is the most alarming aspect of insomniacs. Whenever you have such negative thoughts and feelings of depression arise, the first thing to do is to quickly notice that the negative thoughts are filling your mind: To become aware that I am only filling my mind with harmful thoughts that will adversely affect me.

Additionally you have to drive your thoughts to your advantage. To be specific, you should think of insomnia as a cloud in the sky that will eventually disappear, and that the source will take care of my sleep for itself, that worrying about sleep is as stupid as thinking that the earth and sky will be turned upside down, and that for sleep to return is as natural as nature finding its balance and the universe returning to its original form.

Positive attitudes like leading your thoughts to your advantage are the best actions you can take.

Then, at some point, insomnia switches its course. Your sleep is improved without your knowing.

When positive seed is sown, positive fruit is automatic. This is the truth that you do not have to doubt.

41. Do not be afraid

From time to time, we often have thoughts and react to these thoughts. As long as we live, our reaction to these thoughts is only natural and routine, but sometimes it can be too much. If the thoughts are necessary thoughts you should ponder on them and should not let them flow away without your attention but if those thoughts are trivial or worthless, you shouldn't be too nervous and avoid acting too sensitively.

This is particularly true for insomniacs. They react sensitively to ideas that are useless or overly delusive that pass by their heads and accept them as truths. They applaud themselves for the idea that they will live their lives as insomniacs and that they will not be able to sleep without sleeping pills for the rest of their lives, and with such conclusion already made up, place themselves into the swamp of despair and fear.

Thoughts are not always useful and beneficial. The thoughts that occupy your mind are not always beneficial and you need not react to each and every one of them. Some thoughts are best left to pass by and should not be allowed to be etched in your heart.

If you are suffering insomnia right now then it is probable that the thoughts in your mind are negative. Just as you wouldn't hold onto the clouds in the sky, you should let these negative thoughts pass by. You should not hold onto these thoughts and you should not be afraid of them either.

"What if I don't recover from insomnia?" "What if I live like this for the rest of my life?"
"What if it is really true... ... ?" "What if my life is

ruined forever ... ... ?" The more you are consumed by these wrong thoughts the more these thoughts become stronger and will lead you to the wrongful conclusions that you dug for yourself and will dominate your thoughts.

If you are currently heading this route and hold onto every wrong thought that enters your mind, then it is time for you to stop. By allowing these wrong thoughts to pass by without you clinging onto them will ease your mind and your symptoms will be improved.

42. Enduring mind and understanding mind

Sleep always changes. Good sleep can become bad, and bad sleep can become good. Most people are indifferent to these changes. They know it is not possible to have the same sleep all the time, so they don't react to these changes as drastically.

But insomniacs react differently. They are extremely sensitive to changes in their sleep. And for recurring insomniacs, negative thoughts are that much stronger because of the difficult experiences of their past: Am I going back to the days of insomnia? What if I suffer like the old days?

Such negative thoughts growing day by day they resort to taking sleeping pills, unable to endure the growing despair. They say, "No matter how hard I try, I cannot leave my worries behind."

The reason why insomniacs and recurring insomniacs take sleeping pills is because they can no longer tolerate the bad sleep they experience day after day and find themselves at their wit's end.

If you are suffering insomnia now, it is important not to just endure insomnia, but to understand it correctly. Solving any problems involves understanding the problem.

Understanding the core of the problem – this is the right way to solving problems and insomnia is the same.

43. How to cross the mud patch called sleeping pills

I once consulted someone who takes four pills a day. This man did not even know what medicines he was taking, except that he was taking four. When I checked his medicines, one was a sleeping pill and the rest were antidepressant, sleep inducer and so on. Because the pain caused by insomnia was too much for him he had no more desire to live due to the exhaustion of body and mind caused by insomnia that he did not care to know the contents of his medicines.

No matter how many sleeping pills you take, it is not impossible to reduce them. If you take the time and gradually reduce the dosage, you will eventually be able to quit sleeping pills. However, reducing sleeping pills does not simply mean reducing the amount of the drug. More important in reducing the drug is to reduce the dependency on the drug, which requires you to believe and be convinced that you can sleep without taking pills.

The belief that you can sleep without taking pills cannot be gained by empty advices such as "Do not worry about sleep," "Be relaxed." Such words are useless much like echoes of distant mountains.

To reduce the drug requires your awareness of the life principle, and through it, you should eliminate worry and anxiety of sleep. Awareness of the life principle leads to the faith in the force to care for itself and dilutes the anxiety of reducing medicine.

Fortunately, this particular patient listened to my advice on the life principle, and as a result, the worry and anxiety about sleeping did not increase while reducing medicine dosage. Although actual sleep time was somewhat reduced than when taking higher dosage, his body condition had improved as he was taking less pills. After 20 days, he was able to wean off the medicine and sleep seven hours a day.

Hearing him saying that the world began to look different and that he felt he was being rewarded for the pain he had suffered during the hard times, the idea came to my head that it is not so difficult for us to trudge through the mud patch called sleeping pills.

There are no sleeping pills you cannot wean out of. Many people fail to stop taking sleeping pills because they do not know how to cope with excessive psychological dependence on sleeping pills and psychological anxiety that comes with the break on their dependence, not because they cannot quit sleeping pills.

When quitting sleeping pills, you need a firm determination not to take them and wisdom to remove anxiety and worry of sleep. (The wisdom comes from the awareness of the life principle)

Firm determination to quit sleeping pills and wisdom to rest your worries about insomnia – these are like safe stepping stones that will guide you to pass through the mud patch. If you take your steps aimlessly you will fall into the mud, but if you plant your feet squarely onto these stepping stones, anyone can easily cross the mud patch called sleeping pills.

44. I want to sleep a little longer

There are many who feel they don't get enough sleep even when they sleep much better than before or think they want more sleep. It is a completely human reaction: a kind of greed develops as they fall asleep more easily and sleep better. A little more sleep would mean they'd have nothing more to wish for in the world…

But this is dangerous idea. As soon as you get greedy for sleep, you lose the ability to sleep well. You may think 'I'm not greedy. It's just a little wish.' But that's a mistake. There's no guarantee that you'll be able to sleep as much as you want just because you decide you want more sleep. Besides, the moment you think of it, your apprehension about sleep will sneak in.

Unlike when you fall asleep mindlessly, the

moment you have a desire to sleep more, sleep automatically becomes the subject of your consciousness, and you follow the direction of your sleep until the moment you fall asleep. At that moment, you'll wake yourself up from that sleep. You cannot even enjoy a nice nap. It's all a result of your little desire for a bit more sleep.

The desire to sleep more only ruins sleep, and doesn't help you get more sleep. In the process of overcoming insomnia, you must guard against this desire that many develop without your knowing.

Even if you hang on to sleep, wanting more, your sleep will not improve. The best thing you can do and the secret to longer sleep is to let go of all desires regarding sleep, both big and small.

45. We cannot build a house without a foundation

No matter how impatient you are, you cannot build a house without a foundation. In the same way, you cannot overcome insomnia by simply wanting to overcome insomnia. If you suffer with insomnia and just want a quick fix, it is no different than just building a house and wanting to live in it, not caring whether or not it has a foundation.

In order to live in a new house, first you pour the foundation, build supports and walls, build the rafters, and then fill the house with furnishings. Likewise, to overcome insomnia, you must carefully seek the cause of the insomnia. In your mind, you must build the foundation to solve the root cause, put up supports that will reset the direction of the craving of and the obsession about your sleep, build walls that will not collapse under the weight of the worries, erect rafters that will win over the anxiety and fear of sleep, put on a solid roof created from your innate harmony and balance, thus build a house in your mind where under no circumstance, your comfortable sleep will be disturbed.

Thus, there is a similarity between building a house and overcoming insomnia. No matter how fast you may want to build a house to live in it, it is not possible to build a house that quickly. No matter how fast you may want to escape insomnia, making up your mind that you want to overcome insomnia is not enough.

Just as a journey of a thousand miles begins with a single step, even if you're in a hurry, when building a house, no matter how impatient, you must begin with a foundation. In a similar manner, no matter how desperate the need for sleep, the prerequisite to overcoming insomnia is to let go of the impatient attitude and to build your mind's house with a strong foundation.

46. Escape from insomnia has no relationship to time.

Material gain is directly proportional to time. Even if you stay up all night trying, the time necessary cannot be reduced. However, the work of the mind is not about time. Depending on the level of awakening, the mind is capable of accomplishing a great deal within a day or a moment.

For example, when you fall in love, you can build a house of love in one moment and feel the happiness of love. Your heart which had been lukewarm until yesterday can suddenly become hot today with love for another human being, and fill with happiness heretofore unknown. Similarly, to build a mind's house has no relationship with time. As well, if the house you desire to build is about getting rid of insomnia, as it is a house of your mind, it's possible to build it in just a moment.

To make it all possible, you need the right mindset about sleep. Sleep is a vital function of the body. It is not your thought or will, but rather the will of the source of life that controls sleep. Once such a thought takes over your mind, the insomnia created by the dark side of your mind will disappear instantaneously like morning dew under the sunlight, normal sleep created by the bright side of your mind will appear.

Building a house in your mind has no relationship to time. It is possible to escape from insomnia in a single moment - like a love burning brightly all of a sudden. To be completely truthful, it is total fiction that insomnia is hard to beat, that it takes a long time to beat, and that those who suffered from insomnia longer have an even more difficult road.

47. Constant doubt and anxiety

We believe and trust in our body. Just as the stars in the universe move in harmony, just as nature itself maintains its perfect order and balance, we believe without any doubt or anxiety that our body is in perfect accordance with nature, and that we sleep and wake up naturally.

People with insomnia experience the opposite. They worry not only about things they should not be concerned with, but also about which they must not worry. They observe the natural cosmic phenomenon of sleep, and worry that they cannot sleep as they ought, and are overtaken by fear and anxiety that their sleep won't be what they imagine, To put it simply, this type of behavior toward sleep, which is a natural part of the universal order, is to deny the harmony and balance inherent in the universe itself.

To be anxious and to worry about sleep, which is a natural part of our bodily function, is like worrying that the stars might somehow fall out of their order.

Even if you can't sleep one, two, or even three days, it does not mean there's something wrong with the universe. The universe always balances itself. Even when it seems that the weather is behaving oddly, helter-skelter, it eventually regains its shape. Clogged water manages to find a path. Similarly, sleep, even when it seems so elusive, eventually restores itself.

Sleep is an absolute principle of nature itself, and a natural vital function of the body. There is nothing to add to or subtract from it. It does not require effort and anxiety. When you have a problem with sleep, as long as you don't do something out of the ordinary, sleep will find a place of its own accord as a life principle performing an ordinary function.

Something out of the ordinary is the constant suspicion and anxiety about sleep. It is as if you're trying to fix a cloud in the sky with a pair of tweezers and messing with the order of the universe. Regardless of the issue, suspicion raises suspicion, anxiety causes anxiety, and this way has never been the solution to any problem.

If you have constant suspicions and anxieties about sleep, they are the main cause of your inability to overcome insomnia, and you must know that letting go of these is the key to solving the problem.

48. Too many cooks spoil the broth.

Too many cooks spoil the broth. Too many thoughts can spoil your sleep.

If there's a problem, you must think about it and solve the problem with these ideas. However, thinking doesn't mean you get lost in thoughts. Many thoughts don't lead to a solution to a problem. The key to solving a problem is having that one good idea.

A good thought can turn a bad person into a good one. One good thought can quickly turn insomnia into normal sleep. In order to solve insomnia, it is important not to think too many thoughts but to have one good thought.

The biggest problem for people with insomnia is that they have a lot of thoughts in their heads. When your head is filled with thoughts, it is difficult to fall asleep. Trying to fall asleep while thinking is like looking for peace and quiet in the middle of a raucous market. It is as if there are too many captains wanting to control the helm.

As you navigate insomnia, you don't need a lot of thoughts, just the one thought. Thought upon thought, doubt upon doubt, in the end you need just one thought that will not falter.

"God cares for the vital function of all living things. As He takes of the flowers and the birds, He takes perfect care of all my vital functions. There is no need for me to add worry to it. We must hold tight to the thought that, "To worry about God's work is pointless and pathetic."

49. The power to uproot insomnia

The sea is always changing. It can be calm for a moment, and the next moment, a wave can come up on you. No one can know what will happen at sea. Life is like the sea. A person you loved yesterday can die today. A thriving business can fail all of a sudden. A person that used to fall asleep as soon as his head hit the pillow can suddenly have insomnia.

"I was one of those people that fell asleep as soon as my head hit the pillow. One day, before I knew it, I had insomnia. How is that possible?" But it can happen. What you could not even imagine yesterday can happen today. In life, countless events occur where you wonder how they could have happened.

However, whether sleep comes or goes depends on

the rule of necessity and sufficiency. In other words, if you need to sleep, you'll fall asleep. If you don't need sleep, you won't fall asleep.

It is not up to us to judge whether sleep is necessary or sufficient. That job belongs to the source. Judging the need and sufficiency of sleep is solely the purview of the source.

Because I think I'm the master of sleep, I try to judge how much sleep is necessary and how much is enough. So I fight with sleep. My mind, which is the basis for my sleep, thus, is disturbed. If the mind is disturbed, no matter how much I may want it, sleep will not come.

It's like trying to stop a flag from waving in a windy field. If the wind blows dizzily in your mind, on which your sleep is based, the flag will not stop waving no matter how hard you try.

The way to calm the wind in a dizzy mind is to realize that I am not the master of sleep. It is to know that the master of sleep is the universal life source. When I learn that the power of the source makes me fall asleep and takes care of all of me, the strong wind of my mind will calm down.

When I know the source and believe in it, my mind automatically becomes calm. If my mind is calm, insomnia will disappear automatically.

When I know the source and believe in it, my mind is like that of a child who believes his mother and loves her. When a child believes and loves his mother, and the child is secure in her love and protection, he is always happy and thrives under all circumstances.

Thus, the knowledge of and the trust in the source provide the power to stop the worry and anxiety of insomnia forever. This is the secret to removing the root of all the pain insomnia causes.

50. You think you're wanting and inadequate

When you feel you don't have enough, we do what it takes to fill that void. If it's money, we try to get more money, if it's strength, we seek more strength, and if it's sleep, we try to sleep more. In our pursuit of happiness, it is the most basic human desire to want more and to want to fill a void.

However, if you already have what it is that you want, you don't feel the want or the inadequacy. Likewise, if you already get as much sleep as you want, clearly, you're not an insomniac.

People with insomnia always feel that they are lacking and deficient in sleep, and think they are tired because they didn't sleep well. This is why they are insomniacs. But in reality, they are tired not because they didn't sleep well, but because they're exhausted from fighting with sleep in order to sleep.

It is natural for people with insomnia to feel the lack of sleep and dwell on it, but it is foolish to get nervous about the lack of sleep to the point of getting tired by fighting with sleep. It's nothing but a waste of energy. It causes tension in the body and the mind and is simply a way to interfere with the movement of sleep, which naturally comes and goes.

If you don't try to force sleep and fight with sleep, even if you don't sleep well, you'll be less tired than when you struggle with sleep. Even if you just keep your eyes closed all night, without fighting with sleep, you'll wake up the next morning feeling more refreshed.

The best thing you can do is to accept your sleep.

You accept that you fall asleep when you fall asleep and you wake up when you wake up, be it for a short time or a long time. If you do that, no matter how little sleep you get, the thought that you're not getting enough sleep will diminish, and you won't fight with sleep any longer. As a result, you won't waste your energy fighting with sleep, and you'll feel much better.

Instead of being filled with thoughts about the lack of sleep and ending up tired and weak from fighting with sleep, this way, you'll greet the next day with energy.

51. Street lamp in the dark

"I am standing in the dark now. I cannot see the road at all, and don't know where to go. My great efforts to find the way are not sufficient in this darkness. I take whatever road is at hand, going this way and that, end up somewhere that isn't even a road. Not knowing which way to turn, I just scream in pain."

This is undoubtedly your state of mind, if you suffer with insomnia and experience pain from the inability to sleep day after day.

But in spite of your despair, there is always a way forward in life. Even if there seems to be no hope and nothing more to do, that is just what you think, not the true state of your life.

Once upon a time a girl fell into a well. As it was not a well-traveled spot, the chances of her being found were remote. No matter how much she screamed, no one came, and the girl thought of Buddha, whom she always admired, in this dire situation. She thought: 'I might die here. If I am destined to die, I will die. If I am destined to live, I will live." And as always, she invoked Buddha's name in her mind. That was the only thing the girl could do, trapped in the well.

After some time, a rare passer-by suddenly felt thirsty. He looked around and found the well. Walking towards the well he found, he thought: 'Guess I'm not meant to die!' He was well-pleased with his luck at finding the well. In the well, he found the girl and saved her life.

This is just a story, but in it, there is truth above and beyond.

As we travel the streets in the dark, street lamps

placed at certain intervals light our path. Likewise, there are street lamps along the way when we encounter darkness in our lives.

At such difficult times in life, the street lamps could be: an extended hand of another person; an encouraging word you read when you're at the end of your rope; your mother's long forgotten smile; the strength of a reedy stalk in the face of a powerful wind; the warmth of the sun; or the sheer beauty of a moonlit evening.

If you believe in a universe that has never abandoned a single life, and if you believe that this universe will continue on forever, through this belief, you'll find the many street lamps to light and guide your way.

You must never forget this: when you reach the end of an alley, and you see no way out, unexpectedly, you'll find another alley that is beside the one you were on that you never knew existed. In the midst of your despair with insomnia, you must believe in the street lamps of your life that will light the way you need to travel.

52. No self-fulfilling prophesy

Life is fluid: change is everywhere. All possibilities are open to you. You might be happy tomorrow. You might be unhappy tomorrow. You might sleep tomorrow. You might not sleep tomorrow. You can only know tomorrow when tomorrow comes. No one can predict today what tomorrow will bring.

But with insomnia, you expect the worst. If you didn't sleep last night, you predict that you won't be able to sleep tonight, and you hold on to that expectation: self-fulfilling prophesy.

Sleep didn't make things so, you did.

As long as you expect the worst about your future, and believe it to be your reality, there is no possibility that a different reality will occur. It's as if you wanted to go to the right, but actually chose the left: therefore, you had no option to go to the right.

The one thing insomniacs must guard against is expecting the worst regarding sleep and holding on to that expectation. If you don't have negative predictions about sleep and assert those predictions, you will release the negative binds in your mind, and at a certain point, sleep will re-enter into a normal pattern.

53. How to cross the ditch that is insomnia

There was a ditch running through an old village. Everyone could easily cross the ditch if they jumped over it with a long stride. But being fearful of crossing the ditch, some children fell into the ditch and dirtied their clothes.

The biggest reason for those falling in the ditch, when everyone else easily crossed it, is not that the ditch was too wide or their legs too short, but that they were afraid of falling in before they even tried. The courage to cross the ditch was stopped even before the attempt was made.

Now if you have a ditch of life called insomnia, you must not decide that it's impossible to cross the ditch. Avoid being scared and intimidated in advance. There is no ditch in your life that you cannot cross as long as you don't give in to fear, surrender in advance, or think yourself incapable of crossing it on your own.

Possibility is never born of the thought that something is impossible. Such a thought will result in an impossibility. Whatever the circumstance, if you limit yourself, if you're gripped by the horror of your own imaginings, and think the situation impossible, you won't be able to cross even the tiniest of ditches in your life.

Moreover, the ditch of insomnia is not so wide. Anyone can cross it, provided he doesn't think he simply cannot. The way to cross the ditch of insomnia is just like the way people crossed the ditch in the old village. If you know you must cross the ditch, you forget the fear, and boldly jump over it.

Although it seemed so scary and difficult before

crossing the ditch, afterwards it seemed easier than they'd thought, and it seemed laughable in the end how fearful they'd been. This is what many children got to understand once they crossed over the ditch.

Conquering insomnia seems so difficult and insurmountable before you overcome it. Once you conquer insomnia, you learn that it was easier than previously thought, and quite laughable how scared you were that you would not prevail.

By not being intimidated by fear, by not giving in to despair, or by not giving up on yourself, you can cross over the ditch of insomnia more easily than you might think.

54. Mistakes may pave the way to healing.

There are many that speak of disappointment at the lack of progress with insomnia despite all their efforts and exhaustive attempts. But there is no need for disappointment. Even if you have been frustrated by the many useless attempts you have made over the years while still not solving your insomnia, the process of failing and being frustrated is not so bad in terms of healing. In the end, it may be a way towards healing.

Life is basically a house built on failures and frustrations. If you've succeeded in everything without failure, it means that you have not yet lived a real life. You are in danger of thinking and believing without a doubt that the elephant is a pillar by touching its leg only once.

In life, failures and frustrations, mistakes and

errors are the stepping stones to success and happiness, and are in fact part of the maturing process, not really failures and frustrations. The same is true of failure to overcome insomnia.

If your insomnia is not healed and all attempts to heal insomnia have failed no matter how hard you try, if you realize, through failures and frustrations, that these have been mistakes, this does not put you further from solving the problem, but rather a step closer.

Many only realize through trial and error that their methods have been wrong: sleeping pills are not the way; exercise and food are not the way. By process of elimination, one by one, they find the path to the solution.

Lost among various ways that lead nowhere, realizing you're not on the right path, and thirsting after the right course of action, when you come face to face with the true path, the healing happens instantaneously. It is as if, after a long and arduous meditation, a discipliner is awakened by the ringing of a single bell.

People, who have suffered with insomnia over a long period of time, who have failed with different methods, and now as if grasping at straws, come to me and end their long suffering with insomnia with just one word about the principle of life. This is possible precisely because they have gone through the failures and frustrations.

Mistakes are a pathway to healing. Had there not been mistakes along the way, there would not have been the realization that the path you were on didn't lead to a solution to insomnia.

The power to recognize a mistake as a mistake

opens a new door to healing, and suddenly makes it possible to escape the trap of despair.

55. Problems of waiting for sleep

Life is like a waiting room. We wait for so much in the waiting room of life: waiting for the bus; waiting for a lover, waiting for spring, waiting for success, waiting for the harvest ... For us, waiting is a life in and of itself, and we cannot imagine life without waiting. We are familiar and well acquainted with waiting because we have been living with waiting all our lives.

However, this waiting we cannot remove from our lives, is ironically toxic to sleep. As soon as we lie down, we wait for sleep, if we wake up in the middle of the night, we wait for sleep again...

While waiting for sleep when it's time for bed seems perfectly normal and natural, as far as sleep is concerned, the waiting only serves to drive sleep away.

There is inherent nervousness in waiting. There is as much craving, nervousness, anxiety, worry, and fear in the mind that is waiting and expecting a certain result.

If you have a mind that waits for sleep, the amount of anxiety, worry, and fear will be the same as your longing for and impatience with sleep, pushing away the peace and quiet of your mind.

When your mind is waiting for sleep, there is nothing for you to gain. The more you wait for sleep, the more your mind becomes desperate and irritable. Your consciousness becomes more awake and sleep runs away.

Those desperate to get sleep but cannot fall asleep, no matter how hard they try, don't realize it is they that drive away sleep, and that the cause is their own mind that keeps waiting for sleep. They keep repeating the same behavior one day to the next. As they don't know why, they do the same thing and go around and around insomnia like a hamster runs around a wheel. They don't think they're doing anything particularly wrong since all they're doing is waiting for sleep.

But there is no bigger mistake than waiting for sleep. When you don't fall asleep, you can get up, read a book, exercise, surf the net, and watch television, but if your mind is waiting for sleep even in the slightest, all these activities turn into waiting for sleep, and what you're doing is getting further away from sleep.

If you want to fall asleep, you have to stop waiting. When you stop waiting, the expectations will also stop. When these expectations disappear, the obsessive feelings stemming from the expectations such as tension, nervousness and anxiety will also disappear. Your mind is then relaxed and calm. This is the opposite state of waiting for sleep and creates the magic that brings sleep automatically.

Complete relaxation of the mind is a quick definition of sleep. Everyone's mind, when they fall asleep, is completely relaxed and at that moment sleep comes to them naturally. Therefore, if you do not wait for your sleep, your body and mind will naturally relax, and you will fall asleep: the opposite of the state you were in, waiting for sleep that would never come.

56. Your self-ego is a wall

Basically, the mind is not made of physical matter. It seems to exist but it doesn't really exist and it doesn't seem to exist but it's there, and no matter how hard I try to catch it, it cannot be caught. The true state of the mind is emptiness like the universe. But your mind with insomnia is full of confusion, conflict, worry and anxiety. This is the mind that your self-ego has created.

Your self-ego is always a wall. Just as a wall in space creates a new space, if you have an idea, you are trapped in a prison made from a wall your self-ego has created, separating you from the Divine. The confusion, conflict, worry and anxiety that you experience are the very walls of the prison of your own making.

But leaving this prison is not easy. No matter how

stifling the prison is, no matter how much you want to leave the prison, accustomed to the prison of worry and anxiety, the moment you try to leave, you're gripped with fear: fear of meeting new things away from the familiar: fear of learning the truth about sleep and getting away from the deceptions about sleep. This is the reason it's difficult to overcome insomnia.

Sleep is not a part of our self-ego. The fact that we all fall asleep without knowing and wake up without knowing indicates that sleep has nothing to do with our self-ego. Therefore, calm and comfortable sleep can never come when the self-ego is busily creating an anxious and uneasy state in your mind.

Therefore, when insomnia causes all kinds of worries and anxieties, you need to realize that it is your self-ego's doing, and you need to reaffirm the existence of the source within you. You must accept that all of your life functions are taken care of by the power of the source. This is the point at which you'll break down the walls your self-ego has built and overcome insomnia.

57. The key to getting rid of insomnia - who am I?

Who am I? Here is the key to getting rid of insomnia. In other words, when you know who you are, you automatically escape from insomnia. In fact, this has always happened at my healing center: those who disagree are those who have not experienced it.

Who am I? "I" am usually a member of a family: mother, father, brother, sister, Mr. Kim and so on. I am merely an individual with a name. As such, if you're suffering from insomnia, you cannot even see a foot in front of you from the fear and discomfort, the person you think you are is not the true you.

Whoever you are, whoever you think you are, you are part of nature, and nature is part of the universe. Space with so many different parts is also a part of God. The part always reflects the whole. Part is never just small, weak, worthless, and trivial. The part is the whole and the whole is in every part. That you are part of nature means that you have no less than God's power in you.

The harmonious operation of your body universe is testimony that you have the power of God in you. It is impossible that the only vital function of sleep is out of sync while all your other vital functions are well balanced. Therefore, if you have insomnia and you think you have a problem with sleep, this is only a delusion derived from forgetting the potential power of God that exists within you.

You are part of nature and you have the power of God. You have to be cognizant of this fact. Your true self is not the person who frets about sleep. You have to be aware of this fact. If you think you have a problem with sleep, therefore you have insomnia, and you suffer the symptoms of insomnia, it means you have forgotten that you are part of nature and have the power of God in you.

If you recognize that you are nature, the problem of insomnia is solved easily: just as nature doesn't worry about nature, you don't have to worry about your sleep. By realizing that there's no need to worry, the vital function of sleep inside you restores itself. Insomnia naturally disappears.

58. Correct coping with the negative consequences of insomnia

When you cannot fall asleep and sleep becomes stressful, people search for information about sleep and want to learn how to fall asleep. It is natural that a sick person endeavors to get better, wants to know the cause of the sickness, and how to recover from it. But most similar efforts to try to overcome insomnia end up in negative thoughts and results.

In other words, people look at their problem negatively and fix their gaze on the negative consequences of insomnia rather than seeking a solution in a positive light: a pounding heart, shrinking weight, tired eyes, lack of energy, nervous demeanor… What you see there is not hope of escaping insomnia, but anxiety, fear, and horror of insomnia: like shackles that tie you to

insomnia.

If the results of your research about insomnia bring you unhappiness, anxiety, and frustration instead of giving you happiness, peace, and freedom, you should stop collecting such results, as they won't help you with your insomnia. You must stop holding on to the negative results of your insomnia research and wasting your energy on them. Although no one has asked you to find all this unpleasant material about insomnia, you have gathered it all. It is ridiculous that, having collected it, you look at it while surrendering with a sigh.

There is no reason to own something that will not make you happy to own it. Having something that doesn't make you happy is foolishness.

Leave the junk shop filled with trash about

insomnia and go to the jewelry store full of gold and silver treasures. Enjoy fully the gold and silver treasures that make you feel good just to get a glimpse, and even better when you own them.

The gold and silver are uninterrupted breathing. The gold and silver are a heart that beats constantly. The gold and silver are the ears that hear beautiful music. The gold and silver are a peaceful sleep that comes and goes by itself. They are integral to you, and nobody can take them away from you. Enjoy them fully. That is your right.

The way to achieve a normal sleep is by not surrendering to the negative symptoms of insomnia and realizing fully the truth of life's treasures within us and enjoying them.

59. The attitude of a person who thirsts after sleep

When our body lacks moisture, our body signals thirst, and we drink water accordingly. Drinking water when we are thirsty is an automatic response, not the result of a lot of thinking and worrying.

Our attitude towards drinking water when we're thirsty is totally positive. In other words, when drinking water, we have no skepticism about drinking water and worry about the efficacy of water. Our attitude comes from experiencing and acknowledging the truth that drinking water quenches our thirst, and this faith cannot be shaken under any circumstance.

Whatever thoughts we may have in our head, whatever anxiety we may feel, this drinking of water without hesitation when we're thirsty is the right way to solve the problem of thirst.

The way to solve the problem of sleep is the same as that of solving thirst. Just as you lay total trust in water when you're thirsty, you must lay total trust in the driving force of your body universe that controls sleep.

When you're thirsty, you trust implicitly the water you drink, and you drink it without worry. If you have insomnia, you must trust the power of the source that controls sleep and give yourself over to it 100%.

The power of the source encompasses all aspects and is balanced. The source makes all things grow. The source takes care of your life. This support has no flaws. It always cares in a perfect and complete way.

And in many areas, you already believe in that power. As you drink water without any suspicion, you are entrusting yourself to it. When inhaling, you breathe in without hesitation. When exhaling, you breathe out without doubt. You believe in the power of the source that makes breathing possible without suspicion. It is because of your doubtless faith in such a source that you live and breathe in harmony today.

You must admit that the faith in the power inside you that moves your life is the same as the one to make your sleep return to normal. Your thirst for sleep will be solved by it.

60. The mind that calls for sleep

If you have insomnia, your mind is usually weakened. That is, you have narrow thoughts rather than wide thoughts about your condition and situation. You come to think of restricting yourself rather than liberating yourself: thinking that something is not going well...thinking that you cannot get over the wall...

When your mind is weakened and your thoughts become narrow, and when you worry about deteriorating rather than healing, when you are concerned about limitations rather than freedom, no great medicines, no magic methods, and no efforts can bring about improvement and healing of insomnia. Since the mind is an ingredient in creating the world, thinking negatively with impoverished mind is a crucial move for the improvement of your sleeping problems.

Sleep is not a toy you can play with any which way. No matter how hard you want to control your sleep, you cannot put sleep under your control.

It is narrow, closed, and ignorant thinking to want to sleep as you wish. It is as foolish, reckless and impossible as trying to pluck the stars out of the night sky.

Whatever your thoughts may be, sleep flows along its own path. The way of sleep is to follow the flow of life completely. If you need sleep, you fall asleep naturally. If you do not need sleep, you wake up naturally.

You should respect and accept the flow of sleep, not force sleep, not be afraid or shrink away because you cannot fall asleep. This is an open mind about sleep and one that calls for sleep.

Chapter3, Case Studies of Healing by Life Principle

The examples here reveal the suffering of people with insomnia and the healing process and results. Most of these people found that their insomnia disappeared or improved immediately after my counseling. Of course, the process of healing is accompanied by following the progress after counseling and giving necessary advice, but such advice acts only to calm the ripples after a typhoon has passed.

It is also important to note that, with the exception of a few face-to-face counseling sessions, all others were healed over the phone. Many that have suffered from insomnia for decades are immediately healed and recover normal sleep as a result of phone counseling. The life principle and its truth and efficacy are that strong and definitive. It took a little longer for the insomnia to disappear in those taking sleeping pills, but the effect was the same. All people with insomnia can have the same experience. It is because the essence of life is the same and its function cannot differ from person to person.

1. The case of an elementary student (male) whose insomnia disappeared as soon as he heard my words spoken by another person.

One day a pastor with whom I was acquainted came to me with an alarmed expression. I asked her why. She told me that a child she knew has not been able to sleep for a month. He was in the sixth grade. She knew that I was well-versed with insomnia and asked if there was any way to help him. I was sure I could heal his insomnia. I wasn't sure I could meet this boy and had doubts as to whether he would accept the advice of a stranger he had never met. I had an idea. That was to have the pastor give him my advice in my place. Fortunately, he knew and trusted the pastor.

I said to her, "Pastor, go to him and give him my word. If you give him my word, he will believe it because he believes you. But does he believe in

God?" Pastor said, "Of course he believes. We've talked a lot about God." I said to her, "All right! Go to the child and say this. It's not you, but God that puts you to sleep. When you were little, without being aware, you used to sleep well – it's because God took care of you. Tell him to believe that."

Later, I heard that his insomnia disappeared right after the pastor told all this to the child. It was so natural and yet it left an impression on me. A child who had suffered from insomnia for a whole month was able to sleep upon hearing that God is the one that puts him to sleep!

This is a case where insomnia disappeared quickly in an innocent child by easily believing the truth of the life principle as delivered by a person whom he trusted.

Truth is a pure vibration and every being automatically resonates with the truth.

If the words the pastor spoke to the child at my behest hadn't been true, then there wouldn't have been a resonance in which the transformation could take place. This child clearly shows how change can be created by the resonance of truth.

2. A young mother whose insomnia disappeared after only a phone call (woman in her 30's)

This was a young mother living in Cheonan (Chungcheongnam-do Province). She had not been able to sleep for five months and was suffering with obsession and depression as a result. When she called me, she had been taking traditional medicine for a few months traveling from Cheonan to Seoul, but her insomnia had not changed at all and she was suffering greatly. I fully understood the difficulty of her situation with raising a baby as well. She immediately asked me for counseling. But I hesitated because of the lateness of the hour. It takes more than an hour to have a counseling session. This would mean that we would have to work late into the night. When I hesitated, she implored me to help. She said she was afraid for that very night.

I started counseling her immediately. And I began to explain sleep in terms of the relationship between a car and its driver. As it relates to sleep, our body, from head to toe, is not the driver but the car. What turns on and off the sleep is not the car but the driver, and the vital functions of our body—sleep, heartbeat, breathing, etc.—are the responsibility of the driver and not the car.

The driver of our body takes care of all vital functions of our body perfectly. Who is the driver? He is God. He is the source of the universe. He oversees our vital functions as he oversees all the universes. Regardless of the size of the universe, the principle of the universe is the same. So, you don't need to worry about your sleep, as it is a vital function of the body. Sleep is not the work of car (she), but driver (God).

Listening to me, she told me from time to time that

she understood my explanation well and that she was starting to feel more at ease. Next, I explained about the car's attitude towards the driver. I made her realize that she should not be worried about the car and what she must do is to trust the driver fully, because it's not the car but the driver that takes care of the car. I made her realize also that "I" the car and its various functions, for example, sleep, heartbeat, breathing, etc. are works for the driver and told her that all we have to do is to believe in the driver completely.

About an hour into the phone call, I felt a certain peace in her that was quite different from the beginning of the counseling session. In fact, she told me that her mind was at ease. But I was a little worried and wasn't sure that she understood my words after I hung up. That was because it was the very first time that I counseled someone by phone only. But it was baseless anxiety. Even before I woke up the next morning, I received a text from her. In it, she said that it was morning when she opened her eyes. The insomnia that hadn't been healed even though she had taken a lot of traditional medicine was healed immediately after just one phone session.

This case shows that the effect of traditional medicine is insignificant in healing insomnia. If insomnia was cured by traditional medicine, it doesn't mean that insomnia can be cured by traditional medicine, but rather that your body was in need of such medicine for some other health problem at that time. Insomnia is a sickness of the mind. Insomnia comes from a problem of the mind and it disappears on its own when the problem in the mind is solved. If insomnia does not improve when you take a lot of traditional medicine, it proves that insomnia comes from your mind and you should not try to treat it with medicine. The mind cannot be healed using objects.

3. Meeting of Breathing Law and Life Principle

- Overseas office worker (man in his 50's)

This person was suffering from insomnia while working abroad in Vietnam, heard about my insomnia healing center in Seoul, and placed an international call. As I was worried about the cost of the international phone call and about his suffering from insomnia abroad, I decided to begin the consultation right away, instead of making an appointment for another time. I made him realize how wrong it was to be distressed by insomnia and to be in a state of despair due to his inability to sleep. I explained, using the example of our vital bodily functions one by one, the fact that sleep cannot be controlled by our will.

It was difficult to spend much time because of the expense of the international telephone call. At the end of the 30-minute consultation, I gave him a last piece of advice. I told him to concentrate on his breathing without thinking of other things. I determined that it would be the simplest and the most effective way to remove worry and anxiety about sleep that filled this person's head by focusing his many thoughts on breathing. I showed him various breathing methods such as breathing through the nose, breathing observing abdominal movement. We discussed which method worked well for him on the telephone. He felt comfortable concentrating on the movement of the abdomen. I advised him to focus on the movement of the abdomen with every breath by placing his hand on his abdomen.

This was the right method. While concentrating on his breathing his floating consciousness became calmer, the excessive tension created by worry and anxiety about sleep relaxed, and he fell asleep before he knew it. As he put his hand on his abdomen and concentrated on his breathing, from that day on, the sleep that had eluded him for so long came back to him, and his insomnia disappeared.

This is a case where insomnia disappeared as soon as he realized that his worries about sleep were misplaced, and he redirected them to focus on his breathing. This was a common method for many discipliners. Discipliners are trained to gather many thoughts into one. And by such concentration, they enter a state that is empty of thoughts. That is in fact the goal of the exercise: to enter into a state free of thoughts.

What is Buddha? Buddha is a state without thought. Thus, it can be said that the case of insomnia patients letting go of their thoughts of sleep and beginning to concentrate on respiration is a similar state as that. As we forget our worries and anxiety about insomnia through concentrating on breathing, we approach the state of no thought without noticing it. Sleep is a state of no thought. That's why insomnia can disappear through concentrating on breathing. Of course, it goes without saying that the awareness of the life principle is the basis of healing.

4. Older woman (in her 70's) who recovered from insomnia by thinking of Buddha as the source

An older woman had been taking sleeping pills for 10 years because of insomnia. The problem was that she was taking too many of them. She was up to 6 sleeping pills a day. It was serious. I have consulted with many, but this was the first time I met with a person in her 70's taking 6 sleeping pills every day. I was quite concerned as to whether her insomnia could be healed.

Moreover, more than anything, it was necessary for her to understand the life principle in order to get rid of insomnia, but I wasn't sure that a person of her advanced age could really understand the concept. Also, if she was taking 6 sleeping pills, it wouldn't be easy to get out that habit, so I was hesitant to begin my consultation with her. However, the request from her son-in-law was so desperate that I simply couldn't refuse.

During the consultation, I found out that she had suffered a lot of pain. In particular, she bore a hatred for her husband who made her suffer all her life. It might be cause of her insomnia. I went to work on relieving the pain in her heart. Looking into her eyes, I made her understand that the pain she had experienced was not that she had simply been wronged, but that it was a kind of repaying of debt from previous lives.

I told her that getting slapped for no reason doesn't really happen, as the world moves according to the laws of cause and effect. That she had been responsible for taking care of her family instead of her husband was a way of paying back some debt from a former life. I told her that she was almost finished paying off the debt.

In reality, her life was not free of problems, but compared to earlier on, it was relatively calm. She accepted my words. She accepted that her difficult life and suffering were a kind of debt repayment and that through her ability to endure the suffering and to overcome the difficulties, she has become a better person.

The next task was the sleeping pills. I found out that the six sleeping pills were half-strength. I found out what they were, made a schedule with her to gradually reduce the amount, and asked her to stick to the plan. She promised me to do that.

The remaining problem was the insomnia itself. I decided not to explain to this grandmother the key element of the life principle, the very basic concept to overcome insomnia. It seemed too difficult for her to understand. I decided on a simpler method. She was a Buddhist who even went to the temple occasionally and was devoted to Buddha. I told her that, as in all things in this world that are governed by Buddha, our sleeping and waking are also up to Buddha. She opened her eyes wide, as if she had heard something surprising, and said, "It must be true if you say so."

I asked her to think that she wasn't putting herself to sleep, whenever she was going to bed, but it was Buddha that was putting her to sleep. After that, I kept repeating to her that it was Buddha putting her to sleep. She seemed to believe me totally. In about 20 days, she was able to quit the sleeping pills and succeeded in sleeping well without the pills.

This is an example where I used someone's devotion to Buddha to heal insomnia. What is the right kind of devotion to Buddha? It's not about hanging on to Buddha and wanting Buddha to do something for me, but rather realizing he is everything. In other words, this is Buddha's work, that's Buddha's work, there's nothing he hasn't touched: accepting the fact that all things are the works of Buddha is the right kind of devotion to Buddha. In that acceptance and faith, I don't exist. Without me, the insomnia created by my thoughts could not exist.

This grandmother managed to overcome insomnia, letting go of herself without realizing it, by accepting that sleep is not what she does, but what Buddha does. Unavoidably, it took her a while to stop the sleeping pills, but given her total acceptance of my words, she would probably have recovered from insomnia much sooner, had it not been for the sleeping pills. There is nothing harder in the world than becoming Buddha, but there's nothing as easy as becoming Buddha either. We can become Buddha the moment we accept that all things in the world are Buddha's work. This is quite true of the older woman who recovered from insomnia by believing that sleep is the work of Buddha.

5. Is it possible there's something wrong with my brain cells? – university student in his 20's

This is the case of insomnia caused by the stress of preparing for employment testing. As the stress intensified, he developed insomnia, and he had suffered for about six months. In relative terms, he had not suffered for that long, compared to others. However, he was having great difficulty: just as everyone that suffers from insomnia believes his or her case must be the worst regardless of duration or severity, this was no exception. As his pain from insomnia had become unbearable, he had begun to delude himself that there must be something wrong with his brain.

At his urgent request for help, the first thing I did was to assure him that his own idea that there may be something wrong with his brain due to the lack of sleep was completely untrue, and that as of that moment, I'd never met anyone that had anything wrong with their brain because they didn't sleep enough. In fact, I didn't know if there was anything wrong with his brain in reality, but the idea he'd come up with, that there might be something wrong with his brain, had to be stopped immediately, as it was causing further stress.

I firmly emphasized that there's no such danger, and he does not need to worry about it. Based upon my experience with healing so many, the likelihood of such a condition was nil. My words comforted him, his mind became calm, and his anxiety stopped. After that, I explained to him the life principle and pointed out to him how absurd it was for him to try to exert control over the vital function of sleep.

At the beginning of our session, I felt his mind troubled enough to consider mental illness, but I could feel his anxiety recede as the session was ending. Surprisingly, on the very day he received counseling, he overcame his insomnia and slept for over seven hours. After that, there was a slight decline in his sleep, but it was insignificant. He reported to me later that his mind was at ease with the knowledge of the objective truth about sleep, and he was able to lay down on his bed without any doubt or worry at night.

What is the objective truth of sleep? It is that the vital function of sleep is driven by the life principle and we have no business interfering with it. This is a case where delusional anxiety that there might be something wrong with brain cells due to insomnia disappeared at once by the acceptance of the lilfe principle, and a normal sleep pattern was achieved.

It's possible for anyone to have a bad idea. As

long as we believe the bad idea, it becomes a trap that binds us. But the moment we realize it's wrong, we can escape the trap of the bad idea instantly. This was a good example of how a bad idea can torment a person and how quickly insomnia can be overcome by shattering such an idea.

6. I want to kill myself - office worker in his 40's (male)

This person grew sensitive due to back pain. He also had some family problems. The insomnia occurred as the weather got warmer. As he could not sleep, he went to the hospital and for a time took tranquilizers. He thought that the medication was not the solution to insomnia and came to my healing center, asking for counseling. He hadn't had insomnia for very long, but his anxiety about sleep was considerable. But this is natural. Most people think that their own inconsequential cold is much worse than another's serious disease. He was no different.

As he was taking sleeping pills, I advised him how to reduce the amount little by little and explained insomnia in terms of the relationship between leaves and trees. The fact of having insomnia is like a leaf that feels a little sick, but trying to treat it yourself is like a sick leaf trying to cure another sick leaf: a fool's errand.

He easily understood my explanation that the power to heal insomnia comes from the source, not from him, just as the life and death of a leaf depends on the force of the root, not the force of the leaf itself. I explained that, as a leaf depends on the tree's root system to live a healthy life, people also need to believe in the root system of their own lives to lead a healthy life. This was all over the telephone, but it felt as if he was accepting my words. The tone of his voice seemed clear.

On the first day of counseling, he took fewer pills than he had been, and fell asleep, unlike prior to the consultation, was satisfied with the result. The next day, he called me in a state and said he could not sleep at all and he was out walking around, feeling nervous and frustrated. I could hear in his voice how upset he was. He even said to me that he wanted to commit suicide. I advised him to sit somewhere, not to walk any more in order to calm him down. After he sat down, I listened to him and calmly pointed out what he was doing wrong. And I led him to stop being upset and to accept and have faith in the source.

The counseling was effective and he calmed down, and he was able to sleep well again that night. Even after that, he kept reporting to me about his sleep. He sometimes sent me a joyful text that he slept well. Then I told him to be grateful rather than joyful because joy may excite his body and mind. When at times he was worried that he wasn't sleeping well and woke up often, I made him see that it was not a bad sign, but a good sign that he was improving.

Through this process, he later became aware of the fact that it was his own thoughts that were harmful to him, and he found the strength of his consciousness to make himself feel at ease. Eventually, he started to feel quite sleepy, and fell asleep right away, and succeeded in reaching a state of sleep with no dreams, unlike before. That was just four days after the consultation. It took ten days for him to stop taking the two half-sized sleeping pills.

This case shows that insomniacs suffer as much as to think of suicide. Of course, that was an illusion and a fantasy he'd created for himself. It takes time, different length for different people, to get over their illusion and fantasy. It might take one day for one person, but a lifetime is not enough for another. For him, it took four days.

This person continued to call me from time to time. And he also asked for help as he couldn't sleep again when he wasn't sleeping in the same place. He then lets me know that he was able to sleep well again thanks to my brief advice. As he repeatedly had to go over this recovery process, it made me see how this is similar to a discipliner's journey to contemplation. Life is like peeling an onion. Getting over insomnia is also like peeling countless layers of an onion.

7. It is my wish to sleep well just once before I die (man in his 50's)

This person lost out on much of his life during his 35 years of insomnia. His insomnia started at age 19 and has destroyed his life. Insomnia became shackles for life, marriage, and meeting people. He made every effort to overcome his insomnia: he visited hospitals, did 108 bows every day for two years and so on, but all failed. His life became difficult and a normal social life was out of the question. Although he occasionally drank spiny amaranth tea before coming to my clinic and tried to sleep by using alcohol, curing insomnia had become a bridge too far for him a long time ago.

He was unhappy in many ways and he was unable to tend to his family. With a difficult family situation where he was unable to feel secure became a direct or indirect cause of his insomnia.

After he was gripped with insomnia and wasn't comfortable even for a day, he did a lot of studying to escape his pain. Among those that came to me for help with insomnia, none had studied as much as he had. He pursued enlightenment in the area of religion and had done a lot of spiritual searching. However, he admitted that such study was not effective in healing his insomnia, but instead had become the shackles that bound him to misinformation.

As I started to counsel him, I felt that he understood quite fast, perhaps because he had learned so much through all his pain. When I said something, he understood it almost instantly.

As soon as I said that sleep is not something we can order by our thought and will, but something that the source, root of life does by itself, he immediately says, "Then, there's nothing I should worry about," "That's right. You really have nothing to do. All you have to do is to know that the root of life takes care of sleep, to believe in that life principle, and to put your trust in it." He fell asleep that day. He was changed in one day. 35 years of sleepless darkness disappeared without a trace once the light was turned on.

Looking at this case, I once again confirmed that insomnia is a sort of illusion created by ignorance about sleep. The evidence is that his insomnia disappeared as soon as he was made aware of the right idea about sleep. These dramatic results, the decades long insomnia disappearing in one day and restoration of normal sleep, things he had wished for more than anything, are not his exclusive domain. This result is possible for everyone. As soon as the ignorance about sleep is broken, as soon as we have a correct awareness of the life principle, even insomnia of long standing can disappear immediately. This person is one of those that have clearly proven that my assertion is not false.

8. Sixteen years of insomnia evaporated in one instant – woman in her 30's

This woman had been suffering from insomnia for 16 years. She had experienced sleeplessness in the third grade of junior high school as she was dealing with where to go to high school. She got insomnia again after she graduated from high school and got a job. Her first solution for insomnia was alcohol. Later, she received cognitive therapy at a hospital, and even tried meditation. She also used popular remedies such as drinking milk and using special pillows for sleep. However, all of these methods didn't yield much, and she reached a dangerous state of mixing sleeping pills and antidepressants with alcohol. At that point, she realized she was getting nowhere with all those different remedies, and she came to my healing center.

As I've always felt, those who have suffered insomnia for a long time have a quicker understanding of the truth. It is because they've done all that they can of their own accord and now realize that all of their efforts were mistakes. People who have not suffered as long and who have not yet encountered the wall of their minds still have thick walls of ego, while those who have suffered with insomnia for a long time have a wall of ego that is already breaking down. Looking over her situation, it had been three days since he stopped taking sleeping pills. It was a positive sign that she hadn't taken them for three days, even if she had taken sleeping pills until then. I explained to her the life principle and made her understand that sleep is ruled not by her will, but by the will of the source, she accepted that as a simple rule of sleep.

Healing was quite possible to imagine in her state. Sleeping for more than 10 hours on the very same day of the consultation and sleeping for about eight hours the next day, she experienced a dramatic change where insomnia of 16 years disappeared instantly. The decisive reason for this result was the convergence of her study of the mind and the life principle, and her quick grasp of the life principle as a simple formula for escaping insomnia. Additionally, she also understood why her insomnia was not healed even though she has tried every which way. As she recognized her past mistakes and had no doubts about the truth of sleep, healing of her insomnia was just a matter of course.

Those discipliners who have meditated for a long time realize, once they are awakened, that the truth is easy and uncomplicated. Those who have been suffering from insomnia for a long time go through a similar process. While struggling to get rid of insomnia, seeing that this isn't the way and that isn't the way, once they happen to hear the truth of the life principle, it perks up their ears, and on that path, their insomnia disappears. And they get to know: how easy and uncomplicated it is to escape from insomnia; that it's not hard work and they do not need to look for medicine. As much hardship as you experience in life, you will see life, as much hardship as you experience in life, you will see truth.

9. I know now that it's all about making up your mind - female college student in her 20's

This was a college student. Being a college student, she was stressed by her studies and her career path. Insomnia gripped her after she returned to Korea having spent six months in Spain as an exchange student. At first, she slept for three hours, then for two hours, then for one hour, and finally she couldn't function normally, so she had to take time off from college. She took sleeping pills, received herbal remedies, tried mint extracts and cognitive behavioral therapy in order to heal her insomnia, but all to no avail, and was very nervous and worried.

Her insomnia was not the most serious case. She kept on exercising and was able to sleep to some extent before she received my counseling. Her only problem was that she would wake up in the middle of sleeping. What was wrong was that she often woke up and couldn't go back to sleep. She became depressed and lethargic as she could not perform daily activities.

What upset her was that no matter what she tried, she was unable to find a way to recovery. What she often heard at the hospital was that she should not obsess about sleep. However, there is nothing more ridiculous to say to insomniacs than those words. No matter how much we want not to be obsessed with sleep, the obsession with sleep cannot disappear by hearing those words. Instead of telling them not to obsess over sleep, give them the wisdom to make the obsession evaporate.

One of the most important things that I had to do for this student was to make her feel grateful to get any sleep, be it short or long, and not to complain about the sleep. I emphasized the importance of this, especially when she wakes up in the middle of sleeping. I also reemphasized to her the awareness of the source that take care of sleep. If we are grateful for even a little bit of sleep, the obsession over sleep disappears and our complaints about sleep are also gone. When I explained, through the evidence of pulse, breathing, etc, that all the vital functions of body including sleep are what the source does, her mind desperately trying to sleep was changed to awareness and belief in the principle of life. I also told her to practice sleeping tips 1, 2, and 3.

After she received my first consultation on November 3, she could sleep more and more each day. Her joy at the change of her sleep was revealed by her words, "I know it's all about making up my mind." Yes! Everything in the world depends on making up one's mind.

Insomnia is no exception. Insomnia can disappear only by thinking differently. This student proved it to herself. She suffered the pain of taking time off from college because of her insomnia, but through her pain, she gained a precious awareness that everything is about making up your mind. It seems she gained an awful lot in return for a small investment.

10. It is an unbelievable phenomenon - a civil servant in his 40's (male)

About a year ago, this person got angry because of an unpleasant situation with his boss and couldn't sleep all night. The next day, perhaps because of the lack of sleep, his heart was pounding and he had a headache. He tried to overcome insomnia from that day on, going to the hospital psychiatric department, insomnia clinic, traditional Asian clinic etc.

His treatment included taking four tranquilizer pills and four sleep inducers a day, cognitive therapy at the sleep clinic, and taking Korean herbal medicine to stabilize the nerves. But his insomnia did not improve. He tried everything: exercised, drank jujube tea, and meditated but to no avail.

When he asked me for counseling, he had stopped taking sleeping pills of his own volition but was continuing with taking traditional medicines, eating good foods for sleep, and exercising. As a result of his efforts, he could fall asleep, but he woke up as soon as he fell asleep and couldn't go back to sleep. Even the day before he came to my center, he woke up after sleeping for about 30 minutes and was awake for the rest of the night. But it was encouraging he had stopped the sleeping pills.

The main emphasis in counseling was to control his worry and anxiety about sleep. The same is true of other people, but all such worries and anxieties are caused by wrong ideas about sleep. Just because your self-ego works hard to bring about sleep, it doesn't mean sleep will obey. In other words, we do not fall asleep because we try hard to sleep. Sleep doesn't come from trying, but from a relaxed and comfortable mind.

Absentmindedness was what was needed. When you're absentminded, there is no "I" to try to sleep. There are no intended efforts. However, when insomniacs visit a hospital, it is common practice for doctors to give them sleeping pills, trying to help them relax. This makes no sense. It is only possible to relax using the mind. We take sleeping pills because we fail to relax the mind.

While I was explaining about vital functions and the life principle, he said that his mind was already more comfortable. It was a good sign. As I kept on explaining, his reaction was ebullient. Every time I explained, he replied that his mind felt better. He fell into a deep sleep the very same day he received counseling. He woke up in the middle of the night and was a little scared, but when he remembered my words, he fell back asleep and found that it was morning when he woke up, hearing birds singing.

It was a great experience for him to sleep deeply for the first time since he began suffering with insomnia. He said that it was like he was born again. It was like a war for him to go to sleep every day, but, as the pain of insomnia disappeared all at once, he was indescribably happy.

Even a day earlier, when it was time to sleep, he drank jujube tea, exercised, performed abdominal breathing exercises… With the knowledge of the source, he experienced the disappearance of insomnia, for which he had tried everything but had not happened before: the first thing he did after waking up was to take out the traditional medicine from the refrigerator and throw it away.

It took just one night for him to realize it: he didn't need them! He could get rid of the insomnia using the power of his mind! It was wrong to try to treat the mind by ingesting medicines! Since then, he's been truly happy. He was able to sleep as much as he wanted. But about a month later, he began to worry in spite of his happiness. He began to think that he might not sleep well again. He hadn't meant to think such a thought, but it reared its head anyway.

He had difficulty sleeping once again. Insomnia had recurred. When he couldn't sleep again, he tried to remind himself of my counseling, but there was no sign that the insomnia would dissipate. When he was no longer able to endure the insomnia, he asked me for help again. Listening to the course of his insomnia, I reprimanded him. I told him that all he needed to do was to sleep well and to be grateful for it, and to enjoy it. I told him off for picking at a scab, so to speak, by thinking too much. As I pointed out what he did wrong, he immediately self-corrected and regained normal sleep.

He later said, "I don't know what all those doctors in Gangnam (Seoul) are doing." It was an understandable thought for him: he'd seen so many doctors and had found no hope with any of them. But I know those doctors did their best. But their best is just to take care of the surface of insomnia. It is all they know. It is limiting to try to heal insomnia through knowledge only without the experience of having suffered from the death-like grip of insomnia and then escaping it.

It is like saying we know all about the sea without ever going into the sea. Even if we read books and gain knowledge about insomnia, it is hard to know what is in the sea of insomnia and how to get out of it, based on such knowledge alone. We cannot say that we know the scent of flowers just by reading a book about the scent of flowers without actually smelling flowers. Insomnia is like that.

In this man's case, insomnia disappeared immediately after the first consultation, and then insomnia came back, but my advice about the life principle made his insomnia disappear again. The immediate improvement the second time was due to the truth of the life principle, and the certainty of his awareness and faith in it. Those who have suffered with insomnia for a long time usually have the insight to discern truth or falsehood, and immediately turn to the truth. This person was a perfect example.

11. It's like magic – insomnia has disappeared.- female office worker in her 30's

She suffered from insomnia for about two years. The start of insomnia was due to noise and light coming from neighbors next to and in front of her place. Her place was built in such a way that she could hear everything from next door, to her annoyance. It got to the point that she became nervous and her heart would beat faster as she waited for some other noise, even when there was no noise coming from the next door neighbors.

After about two weeks of suffering with insomnia, she went to a clinic for examination of sleep and received a prescription for sleeping pills. However, whenever she visited the clinic, she became even more anxious and her insomnia was not improved at all because of her anxiety about taking the medicine. Then she turned to traditional medicine and took that for almost 5 months: she slept only a little longer with no significant sign of improvement. She even tried cherry tea and schisandra chinensis tea, all to no avail.

During counselling, I explained to her, using various examples, that sleep is one of the vital functions of the body where humans cannot intervene. And I taught her to let go of wanting to sleep and to become conscious only of the truth of vital functions. That evening, she gave up her regular bedtime routine, such as half-bathing, drinking schisandra juice, listening to meditative music, wearing an eye mask, as she realized these were in fact hampering her sleep instead of helping. She focused her energy on the awareness of the vital functions as I had described to her.

Her focus wasn't so great at first. She kept having other thoughts and then would return her focus to the awareness of vital functions. In this way, she slept from 11 pm to 5 am on the first day. The next day, even her jumping heart disappeared and she slept four consecutive hours without waking up in the middle. The next day, she slept at 11 pm and woke up at 6 am. She sometimes woke up in the middle of the night, but the quality of the sleep had significantly improved. She no longer had the anxiety about sleep or the rapid heartbeat that she used to experience at bedtime.

She was incredulous that this change occurred in just one hour of consultation. But it was for real. She said it was a magical change. This was a case where insomnia disappeared at the realization that the one who rules sleep is not one's self, but the power of the source. Those who take or drink something to promote sleep at this moment should know that they are hidden on the contrary factors that promote insomnia.

To achieve normal sleep does not require special preparation. For normal sleep, we have only to let go of the wrong ideas and wrong behavior. Because she knew this, she stopped taking medicines or taking half baths. As we only become Buddha when we don't try to be Buddha, normal sleep comes to us only when we stop trying to escape insomnia. Whether it is Buddha or normal sleep that you want to achieve, there is one right thought in the mind of those who have succeeded. The idea of wanting to become Buddha or overcoming insomnia is vanity itself.

12. The body can be changed in one day – office worker for 20 years (female)

This woman had suffered from insomnia for five years. Insomnia was caused by work stress, decreased physical strength, basic sensitivity, hasty personality, and lack of confidence in her own body due to indigestion. Insomnia, which started at the age of 40, would last for stretches of months, and became worse in the fourth year. The methods she used were traditional medicine, acupuncture, exercise, cognitive therapy, and counseling at a sleep center. Nonetheless, there was no improvement, and she even ended up even suffering from depression.

When she was no longer able to work, she visited the hospital to get a diagnosis to take a leave of absence, the doctor said to her, "It takes about a hundred days to change a body, but in rare cases, the body can be changed in one day. It happens when a person realizes that what they thought were true and their belief system are faulty and the person accepts that." When she heard this, she doubted whether that was possible. But that is in fact what happened to her.

During consultation, I found out that she had some emotional baggage left in her mind. Since insomnia is partly connected to emotional baggage, I first went about the task of unraveling all this. The best way to dissolve this baggage is by figuring out the cause and effect of the making of this baggage. For example, if someone hurts me, there must be a reason for that: it may be because I hurt that person one day.

If the mechanism for this kind of understanding

works well, the emotional baggage doesn't get filled up, and the accumulated stress can also be easily resolved. I told her about this kind of understanding, then awakened her understanding and awareness of the life principle, and explained that the various healing methods she had used for a long time were ineffective. As I explained one by one each of the vital functions of the body universe, she understood and accepted that the vital functions of the body were not hers to perform but up to the source to perform.

She entered into a deep sleep that night. The moment she opened her eyes the next morning, she realized that a new life was beginning. She was surprised and happy with the remarkable change in her sleep that took place in just one day. Instead of offering her congratulations, I gave her a warning: instead of extreme joy, she should maintain normalcy! And I ordered her to focus on just being aware of the truth. Nothing stays the same in the universe. She slept well today, but there is no guarantee that she will sleep well tomorrow. She listened carefully to my advice that she should be careful of excessive expectations and joy.

My words were etched into her mind and she fell asleep deeply the next day. Her insomnia was over. As time went by, there were slight changes in her sleep, but she was able to sleep very well: no comparison with how she used to suffer. This is a case where the body can change in one day, just like the doctor's prophecy. This is not only possible for her, but for everyone else as well.